MASA

Techniques, Recipes, and Reflections on a Timeless Staple

MASA

Jorge Gaviria

photographs by
Graydon Herriott

CHRONICLE BOOKS

SAN FRANCISCO

Library of Congress Cataloging-in-Publication
Data is available.

ISBN 978-1-7972-0992-0

Manufactured in China.

MIX
Paper | Supporting
responsible forestry
FSC™ C008047
www.fsc.org

Design by Vanessa Dina.
Typesetting by Frank Brayton.

10 9 8 7 6 5 4 3

Chronicle books and gifts are available at special
quantity discounts to corporations, professional
associations, literacy programs, and other organiza-
tions. For details and discount information,
please contact our premiums department at
corporatesales@chroniclebooks.com or at
1-800-759-0190.

Chronicle Books LLC
680 Second Street
San Francisco, California 94107
www.chroniclebooks.com

What makes for the perfect masa?

Since I launched Masienda, a specialty purveyor focused on heirloom masa and corn, in 2014, this question has been at the root of virtually every email, phone call, and direct message (DM) we have received. In fact, that question was the catalyst for creating Masienda itself.

While apprenticing at the farm-to-table restaurant Blue Hill at Stone Barns in 2013, I'd started to contemplate the idea of launching a business in New York City that would be the tortilla equivalent of Tartine Bakery, the San Francisco–based high temple of sourdough. The idea came to me after checking coats and serving drinks to some of the world's most influential chefs and culinary thought leaders—from Ferran Adrià to Enrique Olvera and Harold McGee—at an event on the former Rockefeller estate. On that particular occasion, I played fly on the wall during several of the chefs' conversations about flavor-forward agriculture, the kind that emphasized taste over commodity metrics like yield, and that eschewed conventional farming methods in favor of regenerative organic practices. My mind scoured the possibilities of what ingredients might benefit the most from such a paradigm shift, and corn kept cropping up. Not the sweet kind that we sometimes eat on the cob, but rather the dense, grain kind that makes up cornmeal, polenta, and masa, the dough made of corn that is treated with alkaline water through a process called *nixtamalization*.

As of 2019, a whopping 98.5 percent of corn produced in the United States—that's roughly 750 billion pounds [340 billion kg] annually—went to anything but these food staples. Most corn is a strain bred for nonedible uses, from ethanol to wall plaster to shoe polish and cattle feed. Yet the majority of us happen to be eating the same stuff.

Nowhere was this sad truth more apparent to me than with the corn staple I consumed most: the corn tortilla. From a notably absent sourcing narrative to a flavor that I suspected was well below its truest potential, my store-bought tortillas left much to be desired. Surely, I reasoned, the market had room for a gourmet *tortilleria* fueled by yet-to-be-determined, specialty, heirloom corns—or such was my then half-baked notion of what could be.

At that point, I had zero experience with making tortillas, beyond reheating the "authentic" ones that I used to buy regularly from my local bodega. Nevertheless, I figured that I'd cooked enough personally and professionally to somehow make it work.

In search of a solid gut check on how to make quality tortillas from scratch—but short on paid time off for a research trip—I began to comb the internet. Prominent Mexican cookbooks and bloggers suggested that I first turn to Maseca, the most dominant brand of masa harina in the world.

Maseca is essentially the Folgers or Bisquick of masa. Approached traditionally, masa can take as long as twelve hours to prepare. Masa harina, by contrast, is instant; just add water, mix, and . . . masa.

Like its iconic convenience food equivalents, Maseca's brilliance lies in giving the user a sense of accomplishment from (or illusion of) cooking from scratch. It simplifies the prep, speeds up an otherwise time-consuming cooking process, and makes a home-cooked dish that's nearly impossible to screw up.

Although I have since gone on to build an entire business around cooking corn for masa the traditional way (that is, not Maseca), I'd be lying if I didn't say that I was pretty thoroughly charmed by the stuff at first. During my first couple of tries, I was instantly transported to that feeling of being a kid, making Betty Crocker brownies with my mom. That's to say: pure bliss.

What wasn't to like? Maseca represented a fresh, major step up from the local bodega tortillas I'd previously gone out of my way to purchase. Whereas the premade tortillas had a sour smell and taste from the acidic preservatives, these hand-pressed tortillas were toasty and deliciously bread-like, and I'd made them all by myself! Never mind the fact that, as I'd later learn, my bodega and homemade tortillas were both made from Maseca, or that this wasn't *really* making masa from scratch. For the moment, this was a culinary milestone for me.

My early love affair with Maseca was further enabled by the fact that some of my local taco heroes were using it themselves. During a brief tortilla *stage*, or apprentice-ship, at Tacos Morelos in the East Village, for instance, my teacher romantically described making tortillas as a young girl with her mother in Mexico. Her home-made masa secret? Maseca. In my limited experience, it stood to reason that if two generations of tortilleras used it, surely this had to be the most authentic way of preparing masa and tortillas. So I practiced accordingly.

During the process of building meals around this quick-mix masa base, I'd paradoxically scour the farmers' market for the fresh-est ingredients and spend hours preparing the toppings for each tortilla. But, between sourcing and prep, my masa seemed woe-fully neglected, by comparison.

Which got me wondering: *Is this really as good as masa is supposed to get?*

As I would soon learn, it definitely wasn't. While indeed better than my store-bought tortilla, the Maseca experience still lacked the context I'd envisioned back at my restaurant day job. After all, this masa was made possible by the very same supply chain I was attempting to avoid.

Following months of cooking and research, I finally ended up in Oaxaca, Mexico, the masa mecca of the world. By that point, I'd connected the dots that if I were to make excellent masa, I'd need to start with corn, and if I were to start with corn, it had better be the best corn I could find. Oaxaca is believed by many to be the very birthplace of corn, so it seemed a logical place to begin.

But it wasn't just the promise of exquisite maize that brought me to Mexico; it was, as I soon learned, the manner in which it was cultivated. Throughout the country, about three million smallholder farmers had been practicing the same tenets of sus-tainable agriculture that I'd been in search of; for millennia, they have tended to a rich, biodiverse Eden of corn, with an express emphasis on flavor. It nearly felt too good to be true.

I wasted no time in arranging to meet with potential growers and tasting my way through Oaxaca's Central Valley, ending up in wood-burning, open-air kitchens where farmers' families effortlessly prepared tortillas made from their very own heirloom corn.

Each and every time, without exception, I was struck by the deep pleasure I got from eating these tortillas. While the idyl-lic context certainly didn't hurt, these were, objectively, outrageously good tortillas; decadent, wholly flavorful, and with a texture contrast as satisfying as a fresh-baked baguette. But what was it about the masa that made them so good?

During one of our long car rides together, I turned to one of the agronomists who had introduced me to some of the local corn growers we'd met, and I asked him what exactly made for such special masa. Speaking like a true agronomist, he said that it had everything to do with the agriculture and terroir: the corn was grown alongside key supporting players like beans and squash, which balanced the nutrients in the soil, making for healthy, delicious crops. Partnered with Oaxaca's stunning array of biodiversity, the growing conditions produced an array of flavors that are notably absent from large-scale commercial agriculture. In short, this soil was one of a kind.

This was a familiar narrative that made perfect sense to me; it's why I'd come to Mexico in the first place. But it didn't seem to *entirely* account for this masa's excellence. In my own experience, I had squandered plenty of delicious, well-grown ingredients through technical errors in the kitchen. Certainly, the execution

of these ingredients had just as much (even more?) to do with the finished quality, right?

Back in town, I figured it would be worthwhile to connect with the local *molino*, or mill, where I could learn about the traditional stone-grinding process that I'd missed with my Maseca back in New York. When I asked what made the town's masa so extraordinary, the lead *molinero* (mill operator) proudly extolled the proprietary patterns that he'd carved into his milling stones. This signature design, he said, was directly responsible for the exceptional texture of the tortillas that I'd enjoyed throughout the village.

Now we were getting somewhere! The X factor had to be the stones, which I confessed that I'd never used before. But then there were the cooks themselves, the proverbial abuelas, who'd prepared the nixtamal—the corn steeped in alkaline solution that is then ground into masa. With every tortilla I ate, I'd ask each cook what made them so good. Their answers ranged from their ability to recognize the correct level of doneness of their corn, to the way they hydrated the masa, to their own grandmother's hand tortilla-pressing technique that had been passed down for generations.

The more people I surveyed, both in and out of Mexico, the more diverse the answers became. This was particularly apparent outside of Mexico, where traditions are both devoutly observed but also creatively reinterpreted and remixed across cultures and subcultures. What happens in a third-generation Mexican-American tortilleria in Chicago, for instance, is markedly different from the processes carried out in front of a comal in rural Oaxaca, or an avant-garde Mexican restaurant in Mexico City or a taqueria in Singapore, for that matter.

Individually, each of these perspectives was entirely valid, but eventually I learned that no single approach, region, or culture was a silver bullet for achieving a delicious masa. Together, though, from kernel to masa, they started to tell the complete story of how to create something very special, from scratch.

By the time I returned from my first sourcing trip to Oaxaca, I realized that I had enough responsibility on my hands with building an unprecedented fair-trade supply chain in remote communities scattered about Mexico. So I scrapped my near-term plans for opening the tortilleria of my dreams and reached out to chef Enrique Olvera, whose coat I'd once checked at Blue Hill and who, I'd recently learned, was opening a new concept in New York City called Cosme. Perhaps he might be in need of single-origin, Mexican heirloom corn?

It turned out that Enrique (and soon-to-be hundreds of chefs throughout the international culinary community) wanted masa to be center stage at his restaurant. To do this, he'd need the right partner for purveying corn; not just any corn, but the kind that I'd been working to source from Oaxaca and other traditional communities throughout Mexico. What were the odds? If I could deliver enough supply by the time of Cosme's opening, he assured me, I'd have a committed restaurant partner in the Cosme team. And so Masienda was born.

Since then, Masienda's mission has been to create a new kind of masa value chain, from origin to consumption. Our first step toward that reality was to partner with traditional farmers in Mexico to grow, source, and offer the highest-quality single-origin ingredients. With this unprecedented foundation in place (think third-wave coffee for heirloom corn—for those unfamiliar with the three waves of coffee, see Modern Masa in Three Waves on page 54), we could then set out to serve the masa ambitions of top chefs around the world, including Rick Bayless, Daniela Soto-Innes, Alex Stupak, and José Andrés, to name a few. After beginning with a little over a dozen farmers in 2014, Masienda now supports a network of approximately two thousand farmers across six states in Mexico. As of 2021, we have sourced more than six million pounds [two and a half million kilograms] of heirloom corn grown across regenerative agriculture and injected more than two million dollars into partner communities.

Importantly, while impact-based sourcing is still central to what we do at Masienda, it is our ever-expanding perspective on masa making that is perhaps most valuable to the chefs and home cooks we serve today (hundreds of top chefs around the world and tens of thousands of home cooks, and counting). Until this book, there were no long-form guides to masa making out there. Several titles shed some light on the process but did not break down the seemingly folkloric and ineffable qualities of nixtamalization and masa grinding, or the standard units of measurement and replicable techniques. Instead, much is left to romance and interpretation, without much foundation upon which to build. The proverbial

why—the kind of reflective process that empowers cooks of any level to think creatively and confidently adapt recipes for their own use (especially recipes with intimidating hardware)—is notably absent. Some resources went so far as to suggest that the "purest" approach for preparing tortillas at home is to begin by purchasing the masa from a store, or by starting with masa harina. For understandable reasons of space and focus, to date, an in-depth approach to masa has not fit within the traditional chef/ restaurant cookbook format.

In this vacuum, Masienda has become a proxy virtual message board at the center of the swelling masa conversation. To best serve and anticipate our customers' needs, we have worked directly alongside not just other chefs to understand best practices, but also tortilla artisans in Mexico, third-generation tortilleria owners in the United States, tortilla chip behemoths, molinerxs on both sides of the border, food scientists, academics, corn breeders, journalists, and home cooks. We have launched our own retail tortilla programs across the country, created bespoke in-house masa programs for classically trained chefs, built scalable masa hardware for kitchen use, and successfully worked through tens of thousands of inquiries from home cooks on everything from the best equipment to ideal cooking temperatures and how to prevent a tortilla from falling apart during reheating.

Which brings us to this book. While my journey has been an earnest, even slightly audacious one, it certainly did not begin with aspiring to organize a "definitive" text on masa. To be sure, *Masa* is *not* meant to be anything of the sort.

I am introverted by nature, and the idea of making a statement on the subject—with complex cultural, social, and even political dynamics at play—used to make me anxious to the point of nausea. Despite the fact that my mother was born in Mexico, I sometimes wondered what business I had writing about a cuisine that did not fully define my upbringing, or that of both my parents, or my parents' parents. What would people think when they discovered that the name "Jorge" is not only Mexican? (More on that later.)

As time passed, however, there were three factors that finally pushed me over the edge to write *Masa*.

First, I have a healthy obsession with masa and believe it to be one of the greatest human achievements of all time, right next to the wheel, fire, and domesticated corn. And since discovering the difference of flavor, quality, and experience in the kernel-to-masa process, my vision has been to enable a global masa movement.

The most powerful social movements or cultural phenomena in history were invariably anchored by some kind of galvanizing text, a conscious foundation upon which cultures could interact. But, in terms of masa, there has never been a comprehensive and approachable work to speak of. It is a ubiquitous tradition that has largely survived through oral lore, a brief cookbook acknowledgment here and there, and in some recent, limited cases, rabbit holes on the internet—but nothing more.

The recent surge of interest in craft masa has had the makings of a culinary movement, but it was missing the unifying text it deserved to bring it to a tipping point.

Second, in creating an entire value chain from scratch, I realized that I had a unique opportunity to record, process, and connect the hundreds and thousands of data points I'd absorbed throughout the course of building the foundation of Masienda. These points came directly from Oaxacan abuelas to the largest tortillerias in the world, and from professional chefs to precocious home cooks—none of whom, I realized, had designs or the time to preserve the tradition through a discursive text. And with native languages, cultures, and traditions in direct decline relative to the rise of the globalization, convenience, and, well, Maseca, the future of traditional masa was up against a lot. I felt compelled to share what I'd learned, in support of the art form that made my passion and career possible.

Last, for me personally, there has been no greater way to appreciate a culture than through the sharing of food. The human need for nourishment, and the pleasure that it can evoke, links us all. At its best, it is even capable of bridging differences; it has the transformative ability to build empathy for the "other," in both directions.

Whether we realize it or not, the tortilla is practically more American than a hamburger bun, at this point in our history. It certainly sells more, pound for pound; the global tortilla market, just for context, is expected to reach $48.5 billion by 2023. And within the confines of our current political climate, suffice it to say that it felt fitting to let masa bind us all a bit more—within and across our borders.

And so here you have it, a modern guide to an ancient tradition: *Masa*.

Masa is not strictly Mexican, Central American, Native American, South American, nor is it whatever it means to be American—it is culturally plural. It is the connective tissue between so many cultures around the world, and my intent is to encourage and celebrate that connection with this book. Not only are cultures with an established legacy of masa invited to participate, *all* cultures and walks of life should feel empowered to make this food personal to their respective experiences.

While I can't claim to be composed of any one cultural identity, I appreciate the nuance that exists between cultures. It is precisely because I don't belong to any one place, culture, or tribe that I am reflective about the myriad ways of looking at the same subject. Like so many millennials, Latin or otherwise, I exist at the intersection of a lot of cultures and subcultures, both within my family tree and by the relationships I keep today. My mother was born in Mexico, my father was born in Cuba, and I was born in Miami, Florida. Thanks to globalization and the social experiment that

we call the United States of America, not only do I come from a mixed household of immigrants, my closest friends and chosen family come from vastly different upbringings. All of this influences how I relate to the world that we all inhabit.

While this presence of diversity makes for delicious experiences, it hasn't always been easy for establishing a conventional, straightforward cultural identity. While writing this book, I often struggled with the question of who does, and doesn't, get to write a book on a food that does not completely define their heritage. Am I allowed to write about cultures to which I do not fully belong? I can't decide these questions for you, dear reader, but I *can* share a bit more about my intentions and approach to this work.

For starters, my motivation for *Masa* is educational. As I mentioned earlier, in the years since launching Masienda, my work has afforded me a unique cross-cultural perspective on masa that felt important to share. With this book, my task has been to unify as much of this information as possible, translate it for ease of understanding, and make it widely accessible. My hope is that this project serves as just one example of many initiatives to not only memorialize the collective efforts of indigenous communities, multi-generation tortillerias, artisans, home cooks, and chefs to preserve this ritual, but also to facilitate the continual growth and evolution of this tradition for many years to come.

As for the information on masa itself, I do not claim to own any of it. For this matter, I don't believe that *anyone* does. Nor do I claim to know everything and anything that there is to know about masa, from each and every cultural nuance to all of its possible shapes and forms. There is still so much to learn, and if I have absorbed anything, it's that practice only makes practice. Despite my best efforts to research and compile as much information on the subject as possible, I have not traveled to every single masa-making community in the world (though I've been to more than a few), nor have I met every person, past, present, and future, who has worked with it. By this standard, can anyone really say they've learned everything there is to know? I personally don't believe so, and I hope this book isn't the last of its kind on the subject. As it stands today, it is merely a time capsule of what I have learned—from both observation and experimentation—to date. Nothing more, nothing less.

This book is not meant to try to change or improve the masa you grew up eating or preparing with your family. As far as I'm concerned, there is nothing to fix or do differently. Likewise, there is nothing to alter for anyone's experience that is not yours.

Masa is a food that transcends borders and time; a food that, like corn, has spread itself across generations and cultures throughout the world. It's far bigger than any one place or people, today. It *is* culture itself. And, like culture, it is fluid, ever shifting, and always changing. Every single person can and should approach this tradition exactly as they see fit, regardless of their background.

Masa Basics

What Is Masa?

Masa is the Spanish word for "dough."

If this is your first time encountering the word, you might think that it exists in the Spanish lexicon alone. So widely is masa consumed across the United States and other English-speaking countries, however, that it is also considered an official word in the English dictionary. As defined by Merriam-Webster, masa is not merely a dough, but, more specifically, "a dough used in Mexican cuisine (as for tortillas and tamales) that is made from ground corn steeped in a lime and water solution," through a process called *nixtamalization*.

For the purposes of this book, a modern guide to this timeless staple, written by an American author, we will refer to masa in this English translation, with two modifications: First, while masa's presence in the United States is indeed largely attributed to Mexican cuisine, it is certainly not limited to Mexican culture alone (sorry, Merriam-Webster!). Second, while lime, specifically *slaked* lime, is most commonly used to prepare masa, it is not the *only* alkaline substance used for this purpose. Additionally, this definition begs for the added clarification that, in regards to corn, we are referring to field corn—the grain kind—as opposed to the sweet kind we might otherwise eat on the cob.

Traditionally speaking, masa has been consumed for millennia across all of Mesoamerica, which once comprised the modern-day countries of Mexico, Guatemala, Honduras, Belize, El Salvador, Nicaragua, and Costa Rica. Its presence is also significant in Native American cultures in North America and across Venezuela and Colombia in South America. And at the very moment of this book's publication, through advanced globalization, the masa foodway stretches well across the world (Korean BBQ tacos, anyone?).

So as to not upset any one culture over another, especially with a lack of evidence to support the exact origin story of masa within Mesoamerica, we will assume that masa is culturally agnostic. Be advised, however, that Mexico has arguably the strongest claim to masa, given its prolific history, culinary diversity, and the industrialization of this staple represented within the country.

Further, we will assume that masa encompasses both fresh masa and dry, dehydrated masa, known as *masa harina*. In either such form, masa is essentially composed of corn, alkali, and some degree of water.

Key Ingredients

**CORN
ALKALI
+ WATER
―――――
MASA**

For all of its dynamic culinary range across cultures and recipe applications, the essence of masa is quite simple: Take corn, cook it in a mixture of alkali and water, and grind it into a dough. Unlike its popular sourdough counterpart, no starter, fermentation, or proofing of any kind is needed to make masa. Easy enough, right?

CORN

Before the name *corn*, or the botanical name *Zea mays* (genus *Zea*, meaning "wheatlike grain," and species *mays*, meaning "life giver") was given to this staple, there was the Taíno original name *mahiz*, or Maya *kan*, depending on which of the ancient civilizations of Mesoamerica you refer to. In these early civilizations, even among their descendants today, the belief was that humans sprang forth from corn, and corn itself came from humans. Beliefs such as this were observed in tandem with those that gave life to corn deities such as Centeotl in Aztec culture.

While we can never know for certain the exact origin of maize (that would require excavating every cave and piece of land across modern-day Mesoamerica!), to date we have learned that corn was most likely born in Mexico about nine thousand years ago, somewhere in the Balsas River Valley, particularly within the states of Oaxaca, Puebla, and Guerrero. The highest density of genetic diversity in maize has been found there, which can be linked to foodways around the world, from the Incas and Quechua of South America to the Hopi and Seminole people of the modern-day United States.

Despite much dispute over the last century among archeobotanists, there is now consensus that domesticated corn evolved from teosinte, a primitive grass, though exactly *how* still remains largely shrouded in mystery. One thing is certain: Corn required human intervention to become the plant that we know today. Corn is self-pollinating; however, its seeds are tightly bound to a cob and also protected by thick husks. Even if the corn were to fall to the ground and receive sufficient nutrients and coverage to develop sprouts, the density of kernels so close to one another would prevent it from ever fully reproducing on its own—it needed human intervention to survive.

Considering how instrumental corn has been in not only catalyzing the ancient Mesoamerican cultures to develop from fledgling villages to thriving civilizations, but also spawning thousands upon thousands of industrial products that touch every aspect of our daily lives, it's safe to say

that domesticated corn ranks among the most significant human inventions of all time.

But without the vital process of nixtamalization, wherein corn is steeped in an alkaline solution to draw out flavor and essential nutrients (see page 53), corn on its own lacks significant nutritional value. For this and other arbitrary beliefs held by early colonists and even neocolonial forces in the early twentieth century, corn was improperly considered an inferior food of native origin, low social stature, and economic poverty. Nevertheless, this traditional preparation of corn has not only persisted but also thrived and grown in popularity over the centuries. Even throughout popular culture, present-day chefs are now just beginning to learn age-old techniques perfected in Moctezuma's court. At last, corn's rich cultural value is increasingly becoming apparent to the rest of the world.

LANDRACE CORN

In Mexico, there are fifty-nine (or sixty, depending on whom you ask) core landraces, or breeds, of corn that constitute the basis for the wealth of our globe's corn system. A more specific designation than "heirloom," a landrace is a locally adapted, traditional variety of domesticated species (in the case of maize, a plant) that has developed over time to reflect the natural environment from which it originates.

The landrace is an open-pollinated cultivar that grows through selective breeding. Each planting cycle is known as a generation, and thousands upon thousands of generations can make

up one single landrace seed. Holding landrace corn in the palm of your hand, it is extraordinary to reflect on just how much history and evolution there is to behold.

Within the core landraces, there are thousands of varieties that exist in between. In fact, more than thirty thousand accessions, or varietal samples, have been collected from Mexico in recent decades. So it should come as no surprise that every corn variety—from the otto file of Italy to the yellow #2 and Bloody Butcher of the United States—is a descendant of Mexican corn in some form.

Mexico's fifty-nine landraces are geographically spread out across the country, spanning diverse climates and elevations, and have partly come to inform the very regional cuisines that exist throughout Mexico. Of the fifty-nine, a majority are coveted for their applications to masa, but others are expressly used for other preparations, such as popcorn, baking flours, and sweet corns. A tortilla is different in Oaxaca (a state that, according to Diana Kennedy, doyenne of Mexican cuisine, boasts more than thirty types of corn tortillas) from the tortillas of Jalisco, or Chihuahua, or Yucatán; so too are the corns that make them possible.

Such landraces are maintained by smallholder, mostly subsistence farmers on small plots of land called *milpas*. The Spanish word *milpa* denotes both the corn field itself as well as the complementary cultivation of corn, beans, and squash (also known as the "three sisters" of agriculture). When grown together, each plant fosters

sustainable soil health, and when consumed together, they constitute a fully balanced diet. While some corns may have multiple growing seasons per year when irrigated, for landraces cultivated in rain-fed conditions, each season begins with clearing land (often virgin, especially in tropical climes) and planting saved seed, usually after the first rain in May or June. Corn will develop and dry in the fields until it reaches around 13 percent moisture, at which point the corn kernels are quite tough. From November through January, it is harvested by hand, shelled, and cleaned for use by the entire family. Every part of the corn is put to use, from the kernels (made into masa, pozole, baking flour) to the husks (tamal wrappers) to the silks (brewed in tea) to the stalks (for animal feed). Even spent cobs are used as corks for mezcal bottles, kindling for fire, and are ground into animal feed. After hand clearing the land and a controlled burning of the fields, the farmers create an entirely new parcel and let the former plot regenerate—the cycle thus repeating itself the following season.

HYBRID CORN

Over the last few decades, seed companies have selected certain varieties—both from adapted strains that have made their way to the United States and other parts of the world, as well as by selecting seed directly from Mexico—for commercial gain. This is the foundation of the hybrid seed industry, led by companies like DuPont Pioneer, Bayer-Monsanto, and Syngenta. If landraces are the wild(ish), open-pollinated, variable, diverse corns of the world, then hybrids are the inbred, controlled, high-yielding

offspring of the original landraces. Beginning in haste as early as the 1920s, Henry A. Wallace largely led the way with his company, Pioneer (now DuPont Pioneer), to industrialize corn breeding for commercial agriculture and lay the foundations of today's US agro-industrial complex.

Because hybrid seeds have been inbred over several generations, whether for distinct kernel characteristics (such as less protein, more starch) or plant height (for example, to prevent lodging, or falling over, in the field), they gradually lose their vigor with each successive generation. Think of purebred dogs compared to mixed-breed dogs: purebreds are, on average, more susceptible to breed-specific health vulnerabilities than their mixed-breed counterparts. This loss of hybrid vigor is, at least in part, what gives the hybrid seed industry life; farmers are obligated to purchase more seed, year after year, in order to maximize returns, year after year. The deeper reality, however, is that the act of farmers saving and replanting hybrid seeds is now a crime in much of the world; such agricultural practices constitute a violation of the seed companies' intellectual property, and they are punished accordingly. Farmers, in other words, are locked into buying into the hybrid system.

To be sure, hybrid seeds do produce meaningfully larger yields of corn per harvest, when paired with other inputs that said seed companies *also* sell, such as fertilizers, herbicides, and pesticides. And it is on this basis of performance, cloaked in a grander vision of "feeding the world," that seed companies have, ironically and mostly unsuccessfully, attempted to sell their seed products to the very landrace farmers whose genetics made such hybrids possible.

Among the many reasons that these traditional farmers decline such hybrids and continue to grow their own seed, one consideration, above all, holds the greatest weight: flavor. You see, when characteristics such as plant height or kernels per cob are favored and hybridized, they often do so at the expense of other genes, including but not limited to those responsible for flavor. And while a hybrid seed might indeed limit risk, especially at large commercial scale, it often lacks the culinary backbone that subsistence farmers require of corn, their most important staple. According to one estimate, the average Mexican eats close to four hundred pounds of corn annually. In light of this, corn had better taste as delicious as possible, wouldn't you say?

GMO CORN

A GMO is a genetically modified organism. In corn's case, a hybrid seed alone is not *necessarily* genetically modified, though much of what's grown today is. Hybrids become genetically modified through the artificial introduction of genetics that do not pertain to corn itself (such as glyphosate-resistant properties that facilitate the use of that herbicide in corn cultivation). Some hybrids are GMO, but not all. Some hybrids can be organic, but not all. A GMO cannot earn the title of organic, however, so rest assured that certified organic corn is not GMO. Nonorganic (that is, conventional) crops can be labeled non-GMO, if they indeed are.

CORN FAQ

What is the difference between sweet corn and other corns?

Field corn converts sugars into starch. Sweet corn has a gene that prevents this full conversion of sugar. Field corns do go through a sweet, milky state and are also eaten during this time, shelled and boiled, topped with mayo and lime, or grilled on the cob, or incorporated into atoles or even tortillas (*tortillas de maíz nuevo*).

Can you pop corn that isn't meant for popcorn?

Sadly, not quite. While it may partially pop, it won't yield the same consistency of a true popcorn. You can, however, make nixtamal from popcorn; it just won't perform as well for masa because of the low proportion of the dry white starch. Fun fact: Popcorn is the oldest known corn in the world!

Why are most tortillas made from white corn?

One likely reason is because of a gradual attempt to emulate the appearance of processed wheat flour (both in seed selection and bleaching during the production process), which was considered superior and even mandated by the Mexican government at one point to supplant corn (the initiative failed).

SOFT ENDOSPERM
The starchy main component of the kernel. The more there is, the softer your masa will be.

HARD ENDOSPERM
The hardest part of the kernel where much of the masa's structure and color is derived.

PERICARP
The kernel's skin or hull. When nixtamalized, it helps retain moisture and pliability in finished masa.

GERM
The only living part of the corn kernel, it contains the majority of the corn's natural oils, which are key for emulsifying masa.

TIP CAP
The kernel's attachment point to the cob.

ALKALI

Without nixtamalization, there is no masa, and without alkali, there is no nixtamal.

The term *alkali* refers to a *basic* substance, which is to say one with a pH above 7.

Historically, the alkali used in nixtamalization has been derived from many substances. The peoples of Mesoamerica primarily used (and continue to use) slaked lime, ash, and tequesquite, whereas those north of Mexico chiefly nixtamalized with lye made from wood ash. The Creek and Seminole, for example, employed hickory ash; the Navajo used juniper, and the Hopi fourwing saltbush, or chamiso. Ash was also used for other important purposes beyond nixtamalizaton, including teeth cleaning; slaked lime is a key ingredient in industrial building mortar and cement pastes—which, as we'll learn later in the kernel-to-masa process, is a key binding agent in masa itself.

Today, calcium hydroxide—also referred to as *cal*, *slaked lime*, or *pickling lime*—is the most commonly used form of alkali for the nixtamalization process. It is derived from calcium oxide, which itself comes from limestone that has been heated in an oven through a process called *calcination*. While large commercial vendors sell food-grade versions of calcium oxide, the most common form in which you'll find it across Mexico is solid rock, called *cal viva* ("live cal"). It earns its name because of its live, highly volatile state. Although calcium oxide is safe to use for nixtamalization, it is generally considered unsafe to use it in this unprocessed rock form, as it may also contain toxic metals such as lead or arsenic.

If you should choose to work with it—and certainly enough people use it to suggest that it isn't going to *kill* you—you'll find it mesmerizing to play with, making for a real science experiment kind of moment. To slake, or "cook" the lime (calcium oxide), one only needs to add a few drops of water

Slaked lime

SLAKED LIME Despite their similarity in names, slaked lime has nothing to do the citrus fruit lime (an acid with about pH 2.8). Additionally, while sometimes incorrectly referred to as lye, slaked lime is in fact wholly different. Lye, which can refer to either sodium hydroxide or potassium hydroxide, has a pH of 13 to 14, while calcium hydroxide, or cal, is around pH 12.4.

Tequesquite

WATER

Much like corn, water has a sacred significance across ancient and modern civilizations as a symbol of nourishment, vitality, and life, to name just a few. And, in regards to masa, it is a critical element for not only cooking but also steeping the corn and hydrating the dough that it ultimately becomes.

A masa for table tortillas is made up of about 57 to 70 percent moisture (provided by water), and even a fresh-cooked table tortilla hovers around 47 percent moisture. It's therefore worth noting that water, while seemingly passive or taken for granted in cooking, nevertheless constitutes a significant ingredient in masa. Like a good New York City bagel, masa will react slightly differently when made with various water types—the outcome is never *exactly* the same in each kitchen. For this reason, masa harina producers and tortillerias use highly filtered water in their cooking processes.

on top and let chemistry do the rest. The calcium oxide reacts to the water, steaming as it emits a high heat (up to 500°F [260°C]). Once it's done its business, over the course of 30 to 60 seconds, the original rock will dissolve into a loose powder. That powder is now cal, or slaked lime.

While a seemingly shelf-stable powder, cal does have a shelf life of about one year, following calcination, provided that it is stored in an airtight container. After one year, it is likely that the cal will have lost its potency to some degree.

At home or in a restaurant kitchen, tap water is just fine, of course. Just keep in mind that your municipal water supply has its own characteristics that can subtly affect hydration, texture, and flavor.

LIMEWATER Limewater is considered a medium-strength base that can degrade certain metals, like aluminum. For this reason, it is important to use nonreactive cookware, preferably stainless steel, when preparing nixtamal. As for handling, cal is corrosive and may cause irritation or chemical burns, depending on the duration of contact. Take care not to ingest or inhale it directly, and after handling, be sure to rinse your hands thoroughly.

Tools

TOOLS FOR GRINDING

For the purposes of this book, we'll be focusing on the electric molino, manual corn grinder, and food processor to mill our nixtamal. However, if you happen to have a metate lying around your house, it remains an effective, albeit labor-intensive, way of grinding nixtamal into a masa of your liking.

METATES AND MOLINOS

For millennia, volcanic lava rock, or basalt, has been used in one form or another to grind nixtamal into masa. Given the proliferation of active volcanoes throughout Mexico and Central America, it's no wonder that basalt was so widely utilized. Its relatively soft, porous nature makes it easy to work into various shapes and angles with fairly limited manual equipment. Metates—the slightly concave manual grinding surfaces found throughout Mesoamerica—were widely used for grinding nixtamal into masa, until the application of electricity in the early twentieth century, at which point the electric molino became commonplace. While metates are undoubtedly less common today, they are still used, especially within traditional and/or indigenous communities throughout Mesoamerica.

As one basalt stone specialist in Los Angeles County, Azteca Machine Shop, explains, two kinds of basalt are commonly used in the tortilla industry (which uses mechanized milling, to be sure!): a dark colored-basalt, which has larger vesicles, or pores, and a light-colored basalt, which has smaller pores.

Caused by the gas content within the erupted lava, the porosity of milling stones is critical to their ability to regulate temperature. Mechanical mills turn the stones against one another at high velocities, causing friction, and, ultimately, the transmission of heat, to occur. The larger the pores of the grinding surface, the better the stones' heat diffusion, leading to lower masa temperatures; conversely, the smaller the pores of the grinding surface, the less effective the heat diffusion, leading to slightly higher masa temperatures. Temperature is important, because masa makers want to preserve the fatty oils in the corn and keep them from burning, which would negatively impact the flavor and texture of the masa. For Table Tortilla Masa (page 114), for example, you'll want to ensure that your masa does not exceed 140°F [60°C].

After prolonged use, it is inevitable that particles of the stones themselves will gradually be worn off into the masa over time. This is true for not just traditional basalt stones, but also synthetic stones or the metal plates common to hand-cranked home grinders. Synthetic "food-grade" stones are touted for their durability and slow wear; however, many contain aluminum oxide, which molino purists avoid, on account of personal preference. Basalt, in contrast, is made up largely of calcium oxide and magnesium—alkaline metals that, as Azteca puts it, "naturally run through the blood stream," making it preferable in not only function but also form. As for metal hand grinders, most are food grade and composed of iron and tin, which are considered safe in small quantities (as the trace shavings created during grinding would be).

Whereas the metate and its corresponding *mano*, or grinding rod, are composed of smooth, unmarked surfaces, the circular stones on an electric molino bear patterns across their faces. While many stone patterns follow a roughly similar, spiralized aesthetic, there are variations, both large and small, across the medium. It is an art form and regarded with the utmost secrecy within some tortillerias, the patterns being considered a tortillerx's unique intellectual property (though some seasoned artisans consider this to be a sales and intimidation tactic directed at competitors). Generally speaking, the deeper the lines are cut, the coarser the finished grind. The line depth is largely what distinguishes stones designed for frying tortilla masa, table tortilla masa, moles, and cacao, and is responsible for the most subtle variations with outsized impact.

STONE MAINTENANCE

Volcanic stones—much like handmade Japanese knives—wear over time. If you are routinely cleaning your stones after each use, you'll start to notice a balding on the outer edges of the stones where the previously carved lines are now somewhat, if not entirely, undefined. And if you were to continue using the stones without retracing the lines with a chisel, your masa would increasingly suffer. The dead giveaway is when your masa starts to come off of the stones in gummy, heavy chunks as opposed to snowy, light flakes. I provide some information (see page 252) regarding stone maintenance, including tools and techniques (for example, stone sanding, cutting, repair, replacements, design). For the immediate purpose of identifying variables that will impact a masa's finish (and, in turn, a tortilla's), remember that proper maintenance is as important as the stones themselves.

Stand mixer

Wooden spatula

Fine-mesh sieve

Spatula

Slotted spoon

Measuring cup

Calcium
hydroxide (

Food
processor

molinito

Molino

Spider

Comal

Cuisinart

Thermometer

Digi

Tortilla press

Sheet pan

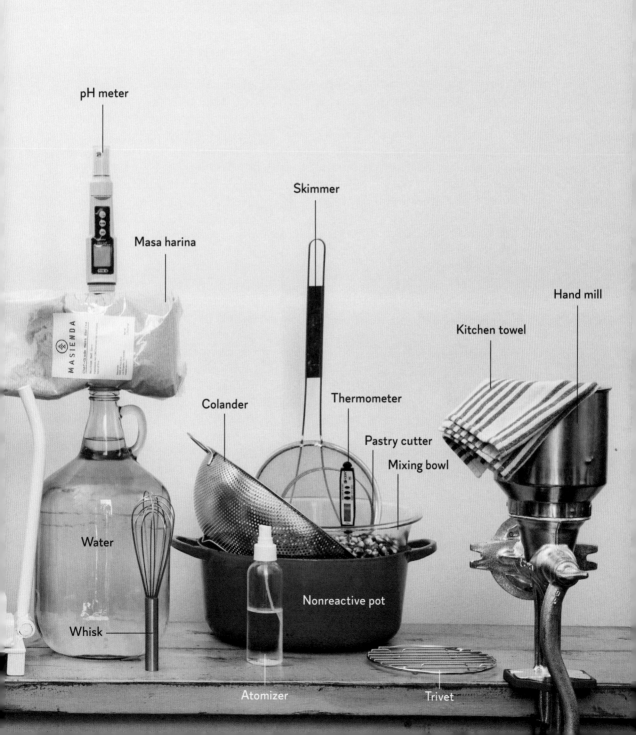

pH meter

Masa harina

Skimmer

Hand mill

Kitchen towel

Colander

Thermometer

Pastry cutter

Mixing bowl

Water

Whisk

Nonreactive pot

Atomizer

Trivet

These patterns were originally carved using hand chisels of various kinds, and some artisans continue the tradition to this day. More often than not, however, stones are carved with carbide-tipped chisels aided by an air compressor or electric rotary saws with diamond blades.

HAND MILL

Hand-cranked corn mills are a reliable, inexpensive, and straightforward alternative to basalt metates or electric molinos. Most are composed of cast iron with metal grinding plates (e.g., iron), in place of basalt. They should clamp directly onto a table for grinding stability, and they are sure to give you a nice arm workout before your meal. There are some electric versions of a hand mill, such as the Nixtamatic from Mexico; however, I have found the manual versions to be far more dependable.

FOOD PROCESSOR

Because so many of us have one at home, I'll cover how to grind nixtamal with a food processor. Bear in mind, however, that this approach requires more water to yield a smooth finish. In turn, this requires either the addition of dry masa harina before use or time in the oven to reduce the high moisture content.

Note that we have not used wet grinders or dry mills to much success, so we will not go into detail about how to use these in this book, nor do we recommend investing in them for this process.

TOOLS FOR COOKING

COMAL

The comal (a word derived from the Nahuatl word *comalli*) is a circular-shaped cooking griddle on which many masa dishes, notably tortillas, are prepared. Traditionally, comales (or comals) are large, handmade, unglazed earthenware disks that are used over a wood fire and, more recently, a gas flame. These comales are quite brittle and prone to cracking over prolonged use, and so must be replaced after a few months (especially if used daily). Because of its porous nature, a clay comal is first partially sealed by brushing the surface with cal that has been diluted with water, then dried over a flame. This not only helps regulate heat but also ensures a nonstick surface, which is essential for any semblance of a tortilla.

While earthenware comales are still used in traditional communities (and increasingly in trendy, cosmopolitan Mexican restaurants), metal comales are most commonly used by household cooks. Often forged from carbon steel or cast iron, metal comales do typically require some kind of oil-based seasoning in order to effectively yield a nonstick surface.

Whether clay or metal, the comal is the workhorse cooking surface of the Mesoamerican family, used for a range of purposes, from toasting chiles for salsas and moles to frying eggs. Throughout this book, we will use the word comal to refer to these more traditional forms; however, it more broadly encompasses and implies any nonstick cooking surface.

DIGITAL SCALE

When working with cal, it's best to be precise. I prefer to use a digital scale that measures in grams, ounces, and pounds, especially when cooking larger batches of corn at a time.

NONREACTIVE POT

You'll need a stainless steel or enameled pot, which will hold up to the highly caustic cal used in the nixtamalization process. A 10 qt [9.5 L] pot should be large enough to cook up to 5 lb [2.3 kg] of corn at a time. The cal may mark and/or stain the pot slightly.

SLOTTED SPOON

As with choosing your pot, you'll want to be sure this material does not react with the cal used in the nixtamalization process. Stainless steel, wood, and even plastic will work just fine.

SPIDER

For use in fried masa applications.

COLANDER

We'll want some form of slotted bowl, like a colander or perforated hotel pan for straining and rinsing our nixtamal.

FINE-MESH SIEVE OR SKIMMER

You can use these for skimming the surface of the water in which your corn is cooking and also for sifting wood ash for nixtamalization.

STAND MIXER

Stand mixers help take the uncertainty out of the masa mixing step—you're sure to get a consistent result every time. If you use a mixer, I find the most helpful attachment to be a dough hook. That said, a mixing bowl and your hands will work just as well. Many have asked if the grain mill attachment to the stand mixer can be used for masa; in my experience, it will quickly become clogged and not function properly. This attachment is really intended for dry grains only. You could choose to dehydrate your nixtamal and grind it into dry masa harina using a mill of this kind; however, the process will require several hours of dehydration.

MIXING BOWL

Stainless steel, glass, wood, or plastic will get both the cal and masa mixing jobs done. The cal may mark and/or stain the bowl slightly.

SHEET PAN

I use a stainless steel or aluminum pan to collect fresh masa from my countertop molino and/or hand grinder. At this stage, the nixtamal you are grinding will be washed, so the interaction of cal with the metal will not be as relevant of a factor.

TRIVET

You can use a metal trivet to prepare tostadas on the comal (versus frying them). It ensures that the tortilla continues to cook and crisp up without charring too much.

How to season a clay comal

Wipe the comal's cooking surface clean with a moist kitchen or paper towel. For a medium-size comal (about 24 in [60 cm]), mix ½ cup [120 ml] of cal with ½ cup [120 ml] of water (that is, one part cal to one part water). Pour half of the mixture directly onto the comal and spread evenly using a dishcloth or paper towel. The goal is to create a uniform, brushed-looking layer across the comal's cooking surface. Add more of the mixture as needed. Heat the comal and brush off any loose residue of cal before using.

How to season a carbon steel or cast-iron comal

Wash the comal with a sponge and soap to remove any residue from the surface. Dry thoroughly and heat over a low flame to ensure that no moisture remains. Apply a thin, even layer of high smoke point cooking oil or special seasoning wax to the surface of the comal (see page 253 for oil smoke point guide). Place upside down in a preheated oven set to between 250°F and 450°F [120°C and 230°C] for up to an hour. Repeat the process as needed.

Note: After using either a clay, carbon steel, or cast-iron comal, do not wash with soap and water. Soap and scouring pads will strip the surface of all that seasoning you've worked to develop, as well as the nonstick properties that came with it. Instead, if the comal is relatively clean, you'll only need to gently wipe it down with a paper towel or dishtowel to remove any excess oil or food bits.

TOOLS FOR PRESSING

HAND PRESS (LITERALLY, JUST HANDS)

The hand shaping of a tortilla is a marvel to witness, as it is, in most cases, the culmination of generations of practice. It is, however, an incredibly labor-intensive process and will likely not yield the desired finish you're after, unless you possess the requisite experience. If you're feeling adventurous, knock yourself out; just don't expect a consistently perfect tortilla (or any tortilla at all, if you're as untalented at this process as I am).

MANUAL TORTILLA PRESS

I always marvel at how such a simple, seemingly straightforward tool can make such an outsized impact on a finished tortilla. It is by far my favorite way to press/shape a tortilla because it provides just enough production consistency, while simultaneously imparting a slightly varied, artisanal look to each tortilla. All manual tortilla presses essentially consist of two flat plates positioned on top of one another and a lever for applying pressure on them. They are joined by a hinge or pivot, which allows the top plate to open up from the bottom and create an opening for loading and unloading the masa. This will be the default method for pressing used throughout this book.

TORTILLA PRESS PLASTIC LINERS

Plastic liners are necessary to ensure that your masa does not stick to either plate of the tortilla press. Cut circular sheets about 8 in [20 cm] in diameter from a thin, plastic grocery bag or gallon-size [3.8 L] food/bread storage bag (the kind without a zip seal). You'll want the liners to be slightly larger than the tortillas you intend to press, so that no pressed masa seeps past its edges. The size of the liners will depend upon the working surface size of your tortilla press. Note: I have found that resealable freezer bags are too heavy and do not easily peel away from fresh masa, once pressed. That said, if it's all you have, a freezer bag will nevertheless be preferable to something like parchment or wax paper, which tears easily under pressure.

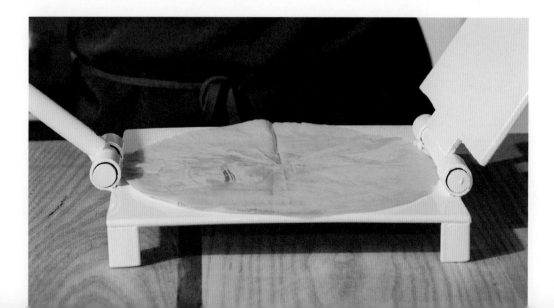

"MACGYVER" TORTILLA PRESS

Two heavy books, cutting boards, the flat bottoms of two pots or pans—you get the picture. Don't let a lack of equipment get in the way of flattening that masa. Where there is a will, there is a way. You'll need the aforementioned plastic liners with whatever you use.

MANUAL ROLLER

This is a relatively inexpensive tool used to create consistent-size tortillas with clean, uniform edges. You essentially feed masa through the top opening, while turning the hand crank simultaneously. The masa is flattened and rolls off the die-cut rollers. In theory, these rollers should work well, but they are often made with poor material and do not produce a sufficient range of thicknesses, in my experience.

AUTOMATIC SHEETER

These are expensive ways to roll out several dozen tortillas an hour. Unless you are serving hundreds or thousands of tortillas a day, this will be overkill. They are, however, effective for larger-scale restaurant or commissary production.

EXTRA TOOLS

TORTILLA WARMER

Whether made from woven straw, palm, or cotton, there are many stylized versions of this tool, also known as a *tortillero* or *chiquihuite*, to keep your tortillas warm. Any clean,

insulating wrapper will do, including a basic kitchen towel.

THERMOMETER

I prefer a laser thermometer gun with a capacity to read at least up to 700°F [370°C]. This tool is especially helpful for reading the temperature of your comal; however, this is a nice to have, not a must have.

PH METER

This is not critical unless you are really wanting to adjust your masa's shelf stability. That said, it's a relatively inexpensive (around $30 to $40) and fun tool to play with, if you are so inclined. Note: You will also need distilled water to accurately run each sample.

ATOMIZER

I keep one of these spray bottles handy whenever preparing masa dishes on a comal, especially a table tortilla. Masa will dry out slightly over the course of your dish preparation. An atomizer, particularly one that has a mist setting, allows you to spray just enough water to rehydrate the masa to your liking.

PASTRY CUTTER (CIRCLE)

Fine-dining restaurants will use these for a more exacting circular tortilla shape once the masa has been pressed into a tortilla. If overlaying a large, decorative piece of hoja santa on the tortilla, for example, a pastry cutter will help trim the leaf and the tortilla to a desirable, consistent shape.

Masa

History

A Mostly Modern Account

I know a lot of us might be inclined to skip over a history chapter in a cookbook.

Come to think of it, I can't even recall the last history chapter I ever saw in one! To be fair, though, I also can't remember the last time I read a cookbook that covered a food staple that is so ubiquitous, yet at the same time underappreciated for the full extent of its role in human civilization.

If you're reading this, then chances are that you've enjoyed masa, in one form or another, for some chunk of your life. Whether you are a tacophile, a pupusa buff, or a tamal aficionado; whether you are preferential to Southern hominy (also known as pozole, which is essentially masa in progress, see page 145), or make the greatest homemade tortillas from Maseca, or are sitting there still unsure of just what masa is exactly, you have good reason to indulge in a bit of history before we dive into our next masa meal together.

That's because context affects the quality of our experiences. And when it comes to a food that we so often take for granted—to which we, as consumers, have historically assigned little to no intrinsic value—how else could we expect to realize that quintessential masa experience without first setting the proverbial table?

Not only does history make for more informed choices in masa or any other comestible, you may be surprised to learn that you are, in fact, part of a cultural movement much larger than your last masa-fueled meal.

Masa Genesis: A Prehistory

As with corn itself, much of masa's beginnings are a mystery. For masa, specifically, we don't know just how long ago the beginning was, and, to date, we don't have records of exactly how Mesoamericans conceived of such a phenomenal, brilliant food.

So far, the earliest evidence of equipment used specifically for masa making was discovered in Guatemala and dates back to 1500 to 1200 BCE. Archaeologists have additionally found earthenware colanders used to strain alkaline chemicals that date back to circa 1000 BCE.

Through such archaeological evidence, we know that the Maya, Aztecs, and others incorporated alkali, a basic chemical compound, into their corn's preparation. They would boil the alkali materials—usually in the form of slaked lime or ash derived from crushed mussel and snail shells or wood—along with the corn in a pot of water. The alkali would help loosen the hulls, or pericarp, of the maize and break down the kernels' cell walls. This process would render the corn's naturally occurring niacin (vitamin B_3) content bioavailable, which is otherwise inaccessible to the human body. Translation: The alkali releases pretty major nutritional goodness.

This alkaline cooking process ultimately came to be called nixtamalization. This word is derived from *nixtamal*, a word in the Aztec language Nahuatl, which itself is a conjoining of *nextli*, or "ashes," and *tamalli*, or "unformed corn dough." Nixtamal is what the corn becomes and what it is called once it has undergone nixtamalization. You may also know it as hominy.

Mesoamericans found infinite uses for this nixtamalized corn, establishing it as the foundation of their diet. From start to finish, they would dry the kernels after harvesting, then cook them in alkaline solutions of varying compositions. Steeping in the cooking liquid for a time not only loosened the pericarp; it also released chemicals that enabled easier grinding and made it less likely that the dough created

from them would tear during the kneading process. The steeping liquid, called *nejayote*, was then discarded, and the corn was washed to remove any trace of its caustic taste.

In their whole state, the kernels could be used in traditional dishes like pozole. Alternatively, when stone-ground with a basalt metate and kneaded into a dough, the nixtamal became masa, which could be made into tortillas, tamales, gorditas, pupusas, atoles, and many other dishes, or used as a thickener for soups and stews.

Delicious recipe possibilities notwithstanding, the development of nixtamalization, along with the complementary relationships between corn, beans, and squash in both cultivation and consumption, is at least in part responsible for the vigor of the Mesoamerican civilization itself. Together with its companion crops of beans and squash, nixtamal staved off diseases of malnutrition such as pellagra, caused by a niacin deficiency, and kwashiorkor, caused by a protein deficiency.

For what it's worth, I personally rank this innovation alongside the likes of fire, the first wheel, and the personal computer on which I write this book today. And yet, despite its potential benefits, when corn was ultimately exported by Spanish conquistadors for global cultivation, they failed to bring along with it the traditional agricultural or culinary processing methods that make it substantively beneficial to human health.

Let's just say they *really* missed out on that one.

Modern Masa in Three Waves

Ever since I first began researching masa, I have been regularly struck by its uncanny historical similarities with coffee.

The origins of both masa and coffee are obscure and shrouded in mystery; they encompass both a commodity and specialty market; they are labor- and time-intensive to process for ritual consumption; their applications are regionally nuanced (think Turkish to Cuban coffee); and they have ultimately managed to transcend the very cultures that gave birth to them, becoming iconic staples of our global pantry, irrespective of birthplace.

Seeing as how most of us have *some* kind of relationship with coffee, I often find it a helpful analogy for contextualizing masa's past and future as a global cultural phenomenon.

Coffee's modern history has been popularly summarized in three distinct waves. The first wave was defined by convenience, consistency, and cost-effectiveness, heralded by brands like Folgers, Nescafé, and Mr. Coffee. Starbucks led the charge for the second wave of coffee, which evolved into much more of a shared *experience* that directly referenced Italian coffee culture; while of a relatively higher quality, the coffee itself was second to the place and vibe in which to consume it. Finally, third-wave coffee focused on an obsessive attention to detail, from direct, fair-trade sourcing to fresh, fastidious preparation. Companies like Stumptown, Intelligentsia,

Counter Culture, and Blue Bottle—not to mention thousands of independent small roasteries and shops around the country—make up this third-wave coffee movement.

While these waves are a progression, they are by no means mutually exclusive. They help delineate how the culture of coffee has evolved in modern times, influencing one another increasingly as time goes on.

So while masa, like coffee, is rich in prehistory, I found it similarly fitting to distill masa's modern history into three acts, or waves, each with a resemblance to its coffee counterpart. By so doing, it becomes easier to appreciate what a force masa has become in mainstream culture, and just what kind of culinary movement we find ourselves in today.

FIRST WAVE: MASA FLOUR VERSUS THE TRADITIONAL METHOD

In the beginning, there was *masa*.

For millennia, this masa was prepared across Mesoamerica using the *traditional method* of nixtamalization and basalt stone grinding.

Up until the early twentieth century, for the female head of each household, every day began with hand grinding the nixtamal that she had started preparing the night before. To do this, she used a metate, a curved basalt milling surface against which she'd grind a 10 to 20 lb [4.5 to 9 kg] basalt rod (a mano or metlapil). To get sufficient leverage over the metate, she'd grind the nixtamal while on her knees—leaning over, arms extended, applying pressure, moving backward and forward for several minutes, or even hours, at a time.

This was core-building and forearm-defining work, to say the least, and afterward, she'd still have to prepare a fire for her comal, portion the masa, and hand press dozens of tortillas (or other masa dishes) that her family would soon expect on the table for desayuno (breakfast). Did I mention that she'd also look after her kids, husband, parents, and in-laws and do garden and home chores, all the while?

Slow clap with me, now.

Because of the masa's high moisture content and lack of refrigeration access (we're going back in time here), it wouldn't hold for much more than

a day without fermenting; the day would therefore end with the preparation of the next day's nixtamal, the cycle repeating itself.

So by the time electricity was leveraged to offset this kind of human labor, you can imagine that metate grinding was especially ripe for disruption.

And certainly, within a few years of mechanical milling's introduction to urban and rural communities, disrupted it was. So much so that these matriarchs could eventually dedicate said nixtamal grinding time to other pursuits. Maybe more time with the in-laws, or perhaps she could try her hand at selling traditional arts and crafts within her community—because, did I mention that she was also an entrepreneur? Whatever the case, she saved time, but not *entirely*.

You see, she'd still have to cook and steep the corn for several hours each day before she could even have nixtamal to grind. Suffice it to say, masa, the linchpin of any and all of her family's meals, was not exactly the most convenient food to whip up when, say, she had unexpected company for dinner (¡Hola, suegros!).

And of course, there was the corn itself, which took *months* to cultivate. While she took care of domestic duties, her husband was busy laboring under the sun. He was tending to his family's milpa, the plot of land where they grew corn, beans, and squash, among other things. The corn he grew came from family-saved seed, passed down for generations upon generations. After selecting from the best of

his harvest to replant the following season, he'd clear a new plot of overgrown land, carefully plant the seeds, wait for rain, weed the parcel, and ultimately harvest his crops—all 100 percent by hand.

Enter masa harina

As Mexico was grappling with the advent of mechanized milling and tortilla baking through the early decades of the twentieth century, first within the capital city and eventually throughout its rural landscape, the seeds of another kind of masa revolution were being sown in the United States.

In 1896, José Bartolome Martinez, a native of Mexico raised in Texas, opened the first fresh US masa mill in San Antonio. It was a hit, to be sure, but he had even greater success ahead. Noting how quickly his fresh masa dried in the arid Southwestern climate, Martinez tinkered with intentionally dehydrating freshly milled masa. At a low enough moisture content, he reasoned, the masa could be safely held for months before use, offsetting spoilage-related losses along the way. And with the simple reintroduction of water and a quick mix, what previously took up to twelve hours to painstakingly produce at home was now tortilla-ready in mere seconds. As for the corn that would go into the dry masa flour, mechanized agriculture in the United States had begun making for a comparatively cheaper raw ingredient at a larger, industrialized scale. It was a breakthrough.

Martinez called his new invention *masolina*, which today we know as masa harina or masa flour. It hit the local Texas market in 1908 and went gangbusters for a few decades.

JOSÉ BARTOLOME MARTINEZ'S LEGACY

Despite Martinez's relative obscurity in the history of masa in the mainstream, his significance to the culture should not be understated. As told in Gustavo Arellano's *Taco USA: How Mexican Food Conquered America*, in addition to inventing masa harina, Martinez even influenced the restaurant offering of tortilla chips and guacamole/salsa, as we know it. Martinez began by repurposing excess masa from each day's production into chips and selling them to local restaurants. As demand quickly grew, he created a full product line around them. He settled on a triangular shape—for their superior scoopability, of course.

Not long after their debut in 1919 under the Tamalina brand, however, Martinez's tortilla chips gave rise to fierce competition. By 1934, a former customer of Martinez, Elmer Doolin, founded a little company called Frito, which in Spanish is "little fried things."

Then came Maseca

Kleenex. Band-Aid. Jell-O. These names are examples of proprietary eponyms. As brands, they have become so successful that their very names are used to refer to the entire class of products they sell.

And yet, while the Tamalina brand may have indeed been the first masa flour of its kind, it's hardly the one that most, if any, of us think of today. In fact, after Martinez passed away in 1924, Tamalina reincorporated under B. Martinez Sons Co., and the Tamalina trade name for masa harina faded away.

Instead, Maseca, a brand that debuted in 1948, became the proprietary eponym for masa and the unequivocal standard bearer of first-wave masa.

Like its coffee analogs of Folgers and Maxwell House, Maseca ushered in an era of convenience, value, and mass consumption. Just add water, hustle, and a "free trade" agreement—with perhaps a heaping tablespoon of corruption—and, buen provecho: first-wave masa.

Maseca's genesis occurred in Mexico in 1948. According to the company's self-published history, Roberto González Barrera discovered a "rustic artifact that was used to grind dried 'nixtamal'" while on a trip to Reynosa, Tamaulipas. Filled with an overwhelming sense of entrepreneurial possibility, Barrera took a sample of the masa produced by the machine to his father, Roberto M. González Gutiérrez. "And together," as the story immediately and reductively concludes, "they achieved a

five-thousand-year technological leap in the industry of tortilla, by changing entirely the traditional manner to prepare the tortillas in Mexico." It was destiny.

The father-and-son duo founded Gruma in Cerralvo, Nuevo León, Mexico, in 1949. Their first plant was called Molinos Azteca, and they named their "revolutionary product" Maseca, whose name comes from *masa seca*, or "dry dough."

Despite the uncanny coincidence of the shared name Molinos Azteca—it is both Tamalina's original founding name in 1896, and the founding name of Maseca's parent company, spawned some forty-one years after Tamalina's rise in the United States—there is curiously no direct connection, competitive or otherwise, between the two companies. In fact, despite evidence to the contrary, with Maseca, the company claims to have founded "the first 'nixtamal' corn flour facility in the world." Such is the power of history's winners.

Revise history as it may, Gruma's introduction of Maseca to Mexico wasn't exactly smooth sailing from the get-go. Much of Mexico had at first resisted mechanized milling, and it gave Maseca a similar early reception. By many accounts, Maseca's flavor left much to be desired—some unimpressed consumers suggested that the insipid flour had been cut with paper pulp. This perception of inferiority was largely attributed to the market's rich history with traditional-method masa, which was still widely produced with diverse and delicious heirloom corns. What Maseca lacked in flavor, however, its makers made up for in patience and political backchanneling.

While Maseca's growth in Mexico remained steady, the untapped US market offered comparatively explosive potential. In 1965, the Immigration Reform Act had catalyzed a mass emigration of Mexicans to the United States. As we'll cover in the second wave, this Mexican diaspora was accompanied by the diverse regional flavors of its homeland, and with it, a massive influence on the broader American palate. And whereas the diaspora itself might have similarly favored traditional-method masa over Maseca, the American standard had yet to be defined. In other words, average Americans, increasingly hooked on Mexican staples, soon presented a massive opportunity for Gruma.

By 1977, the company had begun boldly acquiring small tortilla manufacturers in key regions throughout the United States, converting their production from the traditional method to that of Maseca. Mission Foods was among the early targets, mainly a strategic acquisition as a brand name under which Gruma could sell tortillas made with Maseca to the general American population. Indeed, the brand was quickly embraced by Americans and made meaningful headway into the mainstream. In 1989, Gruma also purchased the Guerrero brand, which in contrast, focused on the Mexican-American demographic. All the while, Gruma continued building its own state-of-the-art masa facilities across the United States, further positioning its now-international dominance in masa flour production and distribution.

The cost of convenience

Meanwhile, back home in Mexico, the stage was being set for solidifying Gruma's undisputed masa hegemony, which it maintains to this day. First up, in 1990, Gruma signed an accord with the Mexican government that would essentially skew the Mexican masa market in the company's favor. The agreement not only limited the subsidized corn supply intended for traditional-method tortillerias but also dictated that all masa market growth be met with preprocessed masa harina. Here, it's worth noting that along with the then state-run Minsa, Gruma was one of the only two masa harina producers in Mexico.

This outcome was no mere coincidence; it was a testament to Gruma's chairman, Roberto González Barrera's deep connections to the Mexican government, specifically Carlos Salinas de Gortari, Mexico's president between 1988 and 1994. In effect, therefore, it had been Gruma that convinced the government to push Maseca-based tortillas instead of those made from the traditional method.

Suffice it to say that Gruma's ties to the government made it additionally well positioned to benefit from the windfall afforded by the North American Free Trade Agreement (NAFTA) that followed in 1994. With cheap American corn now freely flooding into Mexico, Gruma's operating costs certainly benefited, but not without significant social and cultural casualties. NAFTA dealt a massive blow to traditional masa culture.

Through NAFTA, cheap corn made it virtually impossible for small Mexican farmers—the kinds still growing heirloom varieties of corn, or maíz criollo, throughout the country—to compete in price. Emigration of this rural class to the United States surged. Families split apart, often with the males of each household pursuing work across the border. In their absence, local farm output decreased, and with it the biodiversity of Mexico's milpa system. And while this simultaneously lowered total tortilla consumption in the country, Gruma's market share stood to increase overall.

Today, with cheap subsidized corn, advanced proprietary technology, and a chokehold on distribution routes

and retail shelf positions across the world, Maseca is *everywhere*. Gruma has seventy-five production facilities worldwide with distribution across 112 countries and counting. As of June 2020, 63 percent of Gruma's sales and 73 percent of its EBITDA (gross earnings before interest, tax, depreciation, and amortization are subtracted) came from operations in the United States alone. Whether through Mission, Guerrero, or even the seemingly authentic stack of tortillas from your neighborhood tortilleria or local bodega, chances are that Maseca had something to do with your last taco experience.

SECOND WAVE: MASA DIASPORA AND THE EXPERIENCE OF AUTHENTICITY

If first-wave masa was about masa as convenience, the second wave is about masa as experience and authenticity. Let's take it back a second to our proverbial matriarch, whose masa circumstances—early in the first wave—had begun to dramatically change. And let's just say that she had a nephew. His name was Raul Lopez.

Raul was a dreamer. According to those who knew him best, he had aspirations to become a full-time bullfighter. In fact, his passion earned him the nickname of "El Torero" (*bullfighter* in Spanish); he just couldn't sustain a decent living with it. Instead, he got to working with an uncle, who happened to be a prominent molinero in Mexico City.

But Raul wanted more for himself. He was ambitious, after all. So he decided to strike out on his own in the United States. Sure, it was a major transition, and he didn't yet speak the language, but he'd been used to taking care of himself since becoming an orphan at the age of eleven.

Raul moved to the United States in 1942. By then, World War II had already claimed the lives of hundreds of thousands of soldiers, creating a sizable void in the US labor market. Immigrant workers were in high demand, and Raul got a work visa to lay track and load cargo for the railroad industry. Life was fine.

Along with his fellow Mexican paisanos, however, Raul soon realized that he couldn't find a decent tortilla to save his life. Unlike Mexico City, there were no molinos throughout Illinois where he could easily find his fix. Change had been good to him thus far, but no tortillas? What kind of life could he have without them?

Having learned a thing or two about masa from his uncle back in Mexico, he started making tortillas in his spare time, selling them throughout his neighborhood and beyond. Evidently he wasn't alone in his nostalgia for the staples of his homeland. Within a few short years, Raul's side hustle became a full-fledged business, serving the Mexican immigrant community throughout the Chicago area. By 1950, he resigned from his job in order to focus on his burgeoning business full time.

He called his tortilleria El Milagro ("the miracle").

Raul's modest tortilleria would go on to become a bona fide masa empire, a thorn in Gruma's backside, and arguably the most significant force in second-wave masa, to date.

Feeding the diaspora

Like its early predecessor, B. Martinez Sons of Tamalina fame—which, for all intents and purposes, may indeed be considered a pioneer in not only the first wave but also second-wave masa—El Milagro started off by serving the Mexican immigrant community around town. But as this diaspora population grew, so too did its culinary representation throughout the region. Mexican markets sprang up to serve the swelling demand, as did public restaurants hawking regional Mexican specialties.

Of course, before long it wasn't just the Mexican population craving an authentic experience away from home; Americans, too, were now increasingly seeking out "authentic Mexican" in their own backyards. And at the center of each region's thriving Mexican community there soon would be a tortilleria, much like El Milagro, serving tortillas and fresh masa made with the traditional method.

With the exception of lacking the heirloom corns they may have traditionally used back in Mexico, these tortillerias started off as strict adherents of the traditional method, albeit at a slightly larger and more efficient scale. Each day, they'd cook American-grown corn in large tanks over gas-powered flame, nixtamalize with slaked lime, and grind using electrically powered basalt stones.

And with "endless comal" conveyor systems that automated the pressing and cooking of each tortilla, by the 1950s these fledgling tortilla factories could produce a few thousand tortillas per hour.

But as demand increased beyond the tortillerias' local distribution routes, quality was progressively compromised. Preservatives like fumaric acid and propionic acid were introduced to inhibit rapid mold growth and extend tortilla shelf life; and in the absence of colorful corn varieties, due to expense and processing issues, artificial coloring became the norm. By the time Gruma entered the US tortilla market in the 1970s, the pure traditional method that originally defined the second wave was under attack from multiple quarters.

Many traditional-method tortillerias were acquired by Gruma and fully transitioned to masa flour–only facilities. Concurrently, Gruma, having developed its own proprietary tortilla production technology, began peddling its equipment to tortillerias, promising a competitive edge and better margins.

With masa flour, several tortillerias reasoned, labor costs could be slashed overnight and more tortillas could be produced with less space. Consequently, many second-wave tortillerias made the permanent switch. And if the promise of business efficiencies wasn't enough, in some cases Gruma offered incredible incentives to tortillerias to convert, whether through equipment discounts, free product, or even straight cash, according to several industry sources.

Those who were reluctant to convert soon found themselves competing with a lower-cost tortilla. And with Maseca now fueling more and more tortillerias around the country, flavor was increasingly homogenized. Slowly but surely, the American (and Mexican) palate became accustomed to masa and tortillas of the Maseca persuasion.

For many, tortilla production ultimately became less about channeling the experience of authenticity or the taste of home; it became an outright race to the bottom in price. And quality, as you can probably surmise, became the biggest loser. In this evolving competitive landscape, several tortillerias went out of business altogether. Others hemorrhaged cash nearly to the point of insolvency, only to be acquired for nothing by Gruma or private-equity firms. Lamentably, the second wave was punctuated by the gradual extinction of several of its early pioneers.

But not El Milagro.

The new face of mainstream masa

El Milagro, today in its third generation of Lopez tortillerxs, has not only thwarted Gruma's attempts to extinguish or control the second-wave behemoth, but is absolutely crushing it. The Chicago-based tortilleria now counts nine production facilities across the country. Across all of its holdings, El Milagro produces billions of tortillas per year, a majority of which are achieved through the traditional method. In addition to boasting a collection of more than a hundred

different tortilla recipes, they make chips, tostadas, and their very own masa harina for internal use. A seven-decade "overnight" success, they've rightfully earned their position at the top of the US masa game.

But while El Milagro may be closest to becoming the next household name in mainstream masa, it's certainly not alone. A few additional prominent names of the second wave that continue to thrive to this day are Mi Rancho (est. 1939) of northern California, El Popocatepetl (est. 1954) of Chicago, and La Gloria (est. 1954) of Los Angeles. Between the three of them, they'll produce just shy of three billion tortillas per year.

How's that for scaling authentic tradition?

THIRD WAVE: FROM MILPA TO MESA, MODERN MEXICAN MASA AS A MOVEMENT

It's happening.

As sure as the text on this page or the tortilla puffs (page 126) you might have witnessed on the internet: You're smack dab at the start of third-wave masa.

To use a term from restaurant parlance, third wave is happening *á la minute*. Not only is this third progression representative of masa being prepared to order, at peak freshness, right before your very eyes, it's a full-fledged movement occurring in home and professional kitchens across the world, all in real time.

How did we get here?

For starters, despite masa being bigger than any one culture, country, or people, it's impossible to ignore the size and influence of the global Mexican population. If you have eaten masa in your lifetime, chances are overwhelmingly high that your masa consumption involved a dish and culture of Mexican origin.

Further, until very recently, masa consumption was a more . . . shall we say *passive* experience. So if you were to try creating an "authentic" Mexican recipe at home—say, birria, for instance—some of our leading cookbook writers might have included a page or two on how to prepare nixtamal for truly homemade tortillas. But you'd have to imagine that few really believed anyone would attempt the storied tradition of masa preparation themselves.

Perhaps for this same reason, other books would go so far as to abstain from sharing any recipes for preparing traditional-method masa altogether. Instead, they'd suggest, "Go buy some from a local tortilleria, and we'll discuss what to do with it afterward." And if fresh masa isn't an option, "Help yourself to some Maseca." (Never mind that your nearest second-wave tortilleria was likely fueled by Maseca anyway!)

As faithful cooks, we'd come so close to authentically preparing a regional Mexican dish; soaking and frying a medley of chiles for a rich adobo, slow cooking a complex guisado for hours, or manually grinding a salsa verde in a basalt molcajete—only to serve it all on top of a tortilla made with decidedly less effort or character.

Why? we began asking the universe. Couldn't there be more to homemade tortillas than the first- or even the second-wave masa we'd come to rely on?

Speaking for the universe, Google may have answered with a shaky, hand-held how-to video by a precocious homesteader attempting traditional-method masa at home, or an eccentric mixologist's blog entry on kernel-to-masa tortillas. And, while you'd then have some notion that not all masa came from your local Maseca fairy, you wouldn't necessarily be inspired to take the process into your own hands, let alone pronounce the word for the very process that would get you there.

This all started to change, though, once high-profile chefs began to take an interest in channeling traditional-method masa for a new genre of restaurants that would come to be known as *modern Mexican*.

Modern Mexican

Unlike the "authentic Mexican" school that preceded it in the '80s, '90s, and early 2000s, modern Mexican eschewed the notion of "authenticity" altogether. In practice, whereas the authentic approach to a mole, for example, would involve an orthodox observance of the ingredients and processes that might define that dish in central Mexico, the modern sensibility might instead draw on, say, Thai herbs, Hudson Valley produce, and elements of molecular gastronomy technique to achieve a fresh take on the eminent classic. Despite its culturally disparate cues, the modern mole would still somehow taste and look decidedly Mexican, only now it was free from the expectations that its traditional analog should meet.

Dish by dish, restaurants like Pujol in Mexico City, Cosme and Empellón in New York, Taco María in Southern California, and countless others would choreograph a clever dance between modernizing Mexican staples and "Mexicanizing" American classics, all with globally expansive references and ingredients tucked seamlessly in between. At the base of each of these dishes, however, was something at once familiar and completely new to most of us: traditional-method masa.

But wait—this wasn't just any kind of traditional-method masa like that of the second wave; it was one firmly rooted in the ethos of conscious and *active* consumption. Well before their openings, these chefs vowed to forgo purchasing masa and tortillas from their local tortillerias and to bring the process 100 percent in-house. They invested in custom, hulking molinos the size of home refrigerators, complete with basalt stones that they'd somehow learn to carve themselves. And instead of relying on the cheap and abundant commodity corn—even the organic kind—that had characterized the second wave, these chefs placed the same premium on the sourcing of their corn as they did with their locally foraged ramps or sushi-grade Hokkaido scallops: In their eyes, the corn must be nothing short of perfection.

Masa as resistance

From milpa to mesa (farm to table), many turned to Mexico, diving head-first into the genetic cornucopia of the country's surviving traditional milpa systems. Fueled by third-wave masa purveyors like Masienda, land-race varietals of corn were, for the first time, acknowledged by name, provenance, and producer. Like third-wave coffee, this was a completely different sourcing model; rather than aggregating hybrid clones of varietals from large estates or farms across the world, this sourcing focused on the terroir and the smallholder farmers behind each heirloom corn kernel. Once limited to the likes of Ethiopian or Indonesian coffees, "single-origin" had now become a moniker for tortillas too, backed by direct-trade exchanges with subsistence farmers who had surpluses to sell. The one-way NAFTA trade flow of commodity corn had been cheekily turned on its head. Third-wave masa, in other words, had become much more than a foodstuff; it was an act of resistance, a political statement.

To be sure, third-wave masa took inspiration from grassroots movements like farm-to-table and the Sin Maíz No Hay País ("Without Corn, There Is No Country") campaign, established in 2007, and restaurants, in and out of Mexico, that had been producing traditional-method masa in house for years; some, like Oaxaca's Itanoni (est. 2002), had even done the additional work to source diverse materials from local producers of maíz criollo (heirloom corn) since their founding. Notwithstanding all of this, the philosophy, infrastructure, and tipping point of third-wave masa was realized during the emergence of modern Mexican restaurants in Mexico, the United States, and beyond. This can be chiefly attributed to the rise of celebrity chefs and social media, and the ongoing globalization of Mexican food.

Despite its success, third-wave masa began as a comparative challenge and a labor of love for all involved. This kind of approach implied working with tiny lots of diverse material, requiring that no batch of masa be approached in exactly the same way. Shunning preservatives or stabilizers, chefs would need to produce masa daily, with tortillas pressed from hand-portioned masa, to order. Sourced and stored organically, the heirloom corn also carried a higher potential for loss. Delivered in 55 lb [25 kg] bags, it was bulky and cumbersome to boot—it had to be, because these restaurants were now producing thousands of tortillas by hand each day.

As a direct result, restaurant labor and food costs increased, but so too did a mainstream cultural awareness not seen in over one hundred years: The humble tortilla, backed by traditional-method masa, had been elevated to center stage. Oh, and that side of tortillas that you ordered was no longer free—they'd finally earned their own intrinsic value and menu line item at the modern Mexican table.

The results were a marvel to behold. In one early restaurant review of Cosme, for example, *New York Times* restaurant critic Pete Wells waxed poetic about the olfactory pleasures of these next-gen tortillas, comparing the wholesome aroma of these tortillas to a combination of flowers, fresh-baked bread, and a baby's cheek. On the West Coast, the legendary Jonathan Gold praised Taco María for taking their tortillas as seriously as would the most fanatical baking professional. With each acknowledgment in the mainstream, whether by servers in their dining rooms or journalists across all media, these restaurants soon inspired a whole class of modern Mexican restaurants, from fine dining to fast casual, to join the budding masa movement.

Prior to the text you're reading right now, there was no book to turn to for guidance on the subject of traditional-method masa. Instead, these chefs created from a place of intuition, sometimes from memory and almost always from a wellspring of creativity, while also drawing upon each other, their purveyors, and their own inter-generational connections to fill in the gaps in their masa knowledge. And while the results were authentic on the face of it, these chefs were incorporating innovative culinary spins to their masa behind the scenes. Shocking their cooked nixtamal in ice, blending multiple varieties of masa for vibrantly speckled rainbow tortillas, or running masa through cream-whipping siphons for texture manipulation—in short, taking no part of the kernel-to-masa process for granted.

Which brings us all to today. Third-wave masa may very well have begun with chefs, but its enduring presence is attributed to *you*. Full circle, we've found ourselves more curious about the origins of this superfood and more interested in trying to make it ourselves than ever before. Don't believe me? Look no further than your favorite foodie blogger preparing masa on social media, or track the number of hits for "how to make a tortilla from scratch" on YouTube.

Third-wave masa is part of a culinary progression that would have been unthinkable even just a few short years ago. Never has it been easier and more accessible to partake in this movement at home. Just as coffee connoisseurs have embraced the Chemex or burr grinders of third-wave coffee, masa has its own set of tools, gadgets, and now published resources for getting the job done at home. (For a list of exceptional third-wave masa establishments, see Resources on page 250.)

And somewhere out there, our matriarch is pleased that we've found our way back.

>>Late Nineteenth Century

Beginning with steel mills, mechanized corn milling is introduced in Mexico and the United States, to a mixed reception.

>>1896

José Bartolome Martinez opens the first fresh US masa mill in San Antonio, Texas. It was called Azteca Mills (a.k.a. Molinos Azteca).

>>1908

José Bartolome Martinez's "Masolina," or masa harina, hits the local Texas market in 1908 (patented in 1909) and is formally incorporated as Tamalina, under the Tamalina Milling Company, in 1911. Tamalina produces tortillas made with the masa harina and sells them far beyond the state, earning Martinez the nickname "Corn King."

>>1919

Tamalina launches what is considered to be the first commercial corn (masa) chip brand in the United States. The chips are known as *tostadas*.

>>1920s

Tortilla factories in Mexico and the United States adopt automatic conveyor oven systems for producing tortillas at scale. The Sanitary Tortilla Company (a.k.a. Tortilleria Sanitaria) of San Antonio, Texas, for example, is founded in 1925 using equipment of this kind.

>>1924

José Bartolome Martinez dies. Shortly after his passing, Tamalina is renamed to B. Martinez Sons Co., which remains open to this day (as of 2021), albeit as a humble tortilleria in San Antonio—no more masa harina.

>>1934

A former customer of Martinez, Elmer Doolin, founds a company called Frito, the English translation of which is "little fried thing."

>>1948

While on a trip in northern Mexico, Roberto González Barrera encounters a tool to grind dried nixtamal.

>>1949

Roberto González Barrera and his father, Roberto M. González Gutiérrez, found Gruma in Cerralv Nuevo León. Their first plant is called Molinos Azteca, and they name their "revolutionary" produc Maseca, from *masa seca* ("dry dough").

>>1950

Raul Lopez founds El Milagro, a traditional-method tortilleria, in Chicago, Illinois. Other notable second-wave tortilla enterprises— El Popocatepetl (1954) of Chicago and La Gloria (1954) of Los Angeles—are also founded within this decade.

>>1965

The Immigration Reform Act cata lyzes a mass emigration of Mexicans to the United States. This Mexican diaspora is accompanied by the diverse regional flavors of i homeland, and with that, a massiv influence on the broader America palate.

Masa Time Line

>>1970s

Gruma collaborates closely on masa harina research and development with the Mexican government by working with Minsa, Mexico's then state-run nixtamalized corn flour mill.

>>1977

By 1977, Gruma begins boldly acquiring small tortilla manufacturers in key regions throughout the United States, converting their production from the traditional method to that of Maseca. Mission Foods is among the early targets, strategically acquired as a brand name under which Gruma can sell tortillas made with Maseca to the general American population. Mission is embraced by Americans and makes meaningful headway into the mainstream.

>>1989

Gruma purchases the Guerrero brand, which focuses on the Mexican-American demographic.

>>1990

Gruma signs an accord with the Mexican government that will essentially skew the Mexican masa market in the company's favor. The agreement not only limits the subsidized corn supply intended for traditional-method tortillerias but also dictates that all masa market growth be met with preprocessed masa harina.

>>1994

NAFTA is ratified, flooding the Mexican market with US corn. Together with Archer Daniels Midland (ADM) and Wal-Mart, Gruma consummates Maseca's dominance for years to come. Gruma goes public four months after the ratification of NAFTA, and two years later ADM, one of the world's largest food commodity processing and trading companies, purchases a quarter of Gruma's stock. The deal allows Gruma to run ADM's corn-milling operations in the United States while giving ADM increased exposure to and influence over the growing corn syrup and wheat flour markets in Mexico. As for Wal-Mart, the retailer also spreads quickly across Mexico, but its US distribution capacities prove to be too enormous for Gruma's conquering of the United States.

>>1980s–early 2000s

The "authentic Mexican" movement takes hold in the United States, led by influential figures Diana Kennedy and chef Rick Bayless.

>>2007

Sin Maíz No Hay País ("Without Corn, There Is No Country") is founded as a grassroots movement in Mexico, focused on food sovereignty and the revitalization of traditional rural farming.

>>2014

Masienda, a third-wave masa purveyor, launches in the United States, serving chefs and home cooks around the world with single-origin ingredients, tools, and resources for preparing masa from scratch.

to Masa

The Process

In this section, I have drawn on every encounter and experience that I have ever had with masa experts and enthusiasts from across the world and pieced the best practices together into a clear, consistent approach for achieving your own personal vision of masa perfection.

When it comes to teaching about masa, I have always found it helpful to think about the common cup of coffee. If you have ever prepared coffee, which I imagine most folks reading this have, you'll know that there are countless ways to prepare that cup of joe. And while a drip coffee may be your go-to way to wake up in the morning, there may be an occasion every so often where an espresso or a cold brew is the only thing that hits the spot. Each method is not more or less right than the other; rather, they represent a range of potential coffee-making techniques from which to choose.

As our friends at Counter Culture Coffee—one of the early pioneers of gourmet, third-wave coffee—teach their aspiring barista students, brewing good coffee is all about knowing the variables and adjusting them to suit your definition of delicious. Making masa is the same deal, and together, we'll unpack the ways to arrive at what ultimately satisfies your own cravings and culinary curiosities.

If you would prefer to jump right into an abridged recipe for masa making, you may skip to page 114 for Table Tortilla Masa.

If you would prefer to jump right into an abridged recipe for masa making, you may skip to page 114 for Table Tortilla Masa.

STEP 1

Precooking (It's Really a Step, so Stay with Me)

Let's start this step with a simple ice breaker:

What is the best masa dish you have ever had?

Masa is a component of literally hundreds of unique dishes, some of which suit our tastes more than others, perhaps. So take a moment to think about what that dish was—or better yet, what it *might* be, if you were to prepare it for your next meal. If it's a tortilla, is it a soft, warm, pillowy one that puffed as it cooked, or is it the kind that crisped up in the fryer for a crackling, salty, decadent tostada?

Maybe it's a tamal? Does the very mention of that dish make you think of the cakey, delightfully spongy kind with braised vegetables or meat inside, or is it the dense, almost fudge-like version that is commonly wrapped and steamed in banana leaves?

The first step before cooking, then, is to begin with the end in (your) mind. What will the final application be? Is your goal a table tortilla or a tortilla for frying? (Yes, there is a difference—as you'll see on page 111!) Will the tortillas be consumed immediately or stored for several days? Each step in the kernel-to-masa process may look slightly different from dish to dish, so the destination will serve to inform the journey.

Regardless of the application, as the name of this section implies, we are starting with kernels of dry corn and transforming them, step by step, into the masa dish of your preference. Let's therefore make sure that we cover the basic technical cooking considerations of our fundamental star ingredient: corn.

PRECOOK CONSIDERATIONS
Consider the moisture content

Along with my love affair with tortillas, I've long been enamored with pasta, especially dry pasta. Understanding the difference between a fresh noodle (a 2- to 4-minute boil) and a dry noodle (a 7- to 15-minute boil) helped me appreciate how even one to two percentage points in a corn

kernel's moisture level can potentially affect batch cooking and steeping times. You would be ill-advised to cook a dry strand of spaghetti for as little time as a fresh raviolo, for example; similarly, you shouldn't approach two varieties of corn in the exact same way.

For the over-achieving home cooks and industry folks: Depending on the size and sophistication of the company selling you the corn, you can usually just ask what the moisture content is for that specific lot. Virtually all corn sold in the United States is at or just below 15 percent moisture, which is low enough to discourage mold growth but high enough to cushion the kernel from physical damage in processing and transit. Some may be dried down to 12 percent moisture and reach as low as 11 percent before use. Moisture can have an outsize impact on cooking time, especially when dealing with large volumes. For a high-volume tortilleria built for speed and efficiency, an 11 percent average moisture could require an unsustainably longer cooking process that costs more in inputs like gas and electricity. Conversely, a home cook with all the time in the world may appreciate the unit value of a drier corn kernel (more bang for your buck!).

For the rest of us: Look, even if you don't bother determining the moisture content, remember that no two things in nature are exactly the same, no matter how controlled the environment or genetics, so cooking times will be affected accordingly. If you've ever cooked dry beans, you've probably already experienced these subtleties in moisture without even realizing it. And in those instances,

I'd bet that you did what any capable cook does and simply tasted for the right level of doneness throughout the cooking process. We'll be taking that same approach with corn for masa, so don't be intimidated by this new input of knowledge.

Consider the kernel starch density

Again, there are lab analyses that can provide this information, but they are a little harder to come by—and slightly more confusing—than basic moisture readings.

Alternatively, I use two simpler methods: sight and feel. Visually, how large or small is the kernel? Does it look dense and compact or big and floury? As for feel, by cracking a kernel with the back of your teeth (or, carefully, with a knife, as my dentist has urged me to do) and swirling the starch around, you can get a general sense of how quickly or slowly the corn will cook.

Cross sections displaying hard (*bolita, left*) and soft (*cónico, right*) starch density examples.

If it's harder in its raw state (typical of the bolita varietal, for example), you'll want to give it more time; if it's a softer variety, like cónico, perhaps less.

The more often you inspect and taste a raw corn kernel, the more perspective you'll gain regarding what different varietals have to offer. Creating tasting references, from kernel to masa, will only strengthen your command of the entire process.

Consider the source

I encourage you to explore where your food comes from whenever possible. I'm not saying that you need to go *Portlandia* on your ingredients—memorizing the corn's name and surveying its farmers on whether it had a happy life in the fields is not necessary—but remember that the source of your corn will have a lot to do with your resulting masa.

Most corn companies in the United States rely on hybrid varieties, which means they have been through countless generations of breeding for very specific purposes. What's more, we don't always know whether we're buying a hybrid variety that would not best serve our end masa goal. A portion of the generic blue corn (even the non-GMO and organic stuff) available in the United States, for example, is designed for chips. These grain types with denser starches are less likely to absorb excess oil, which is less important for table tortilla masa. This doesn't mean that all blue corn is better for chips, or that you can't make a tortilla from blue corn that was bred to produce chips. It simply means that the hybrid you may be using was perhaps designed with a different goal in mind.

It's helpful, also, to be aware that commercial agriculture and the masa industry are built upon increasingly concentrated ownership and narrowing genetic variation. This means there's not a lot of corn variety to choose from, as a home or restaurant consumer, unless you branch out from these conventional systems. This is what makes working at the source in Mexico so exciting—there are tens of thousands of variations to choose from and enjoy. Every kernel or lot may have subtle differences to note, but with a basic understanding of these precook variables, you'll know how to dial into exactly what you're looking for in your masa.

All things considered

All corn—just like all other grains, fruits, vegetables, and so on—is not created equal. Diversity is delicious. Play to your preferences. There's plenty of great stuff to choose from out there.

STEP 2

Cooking with Cal

Cooking is both a precursor to, and integral part of, nixtamalization. It's hard to talk about cooking without mentioning what comes next in the sequence—after all, cooking and nixtamalization do have some chronological overlap. Because of the implications of its function, however, I wanted to be sure to make this a standalone step for the corn cook.

Most folks who have cooked in their lifetimes have yet to do so with calcium hydroxide. I get it. This can be intimidating for many. It was for me, when I first got started, well before I could even pronounce nixtamalization. But even if you're in that camp, trust me: You've got this.

Have you ever boiled an egg? Broccoli? Pasta? This is literally the same process, but instead of using just water (or salted water), we're adding cal to the mix. It's actually that simple. And even if you've never cooked any of those foods (or anything ever!), I still have you covered.

WHY WE COOK WITH CAL
Make the corn palatable

Like with any food, cooking—in this case through the introduction of heat that is conducted through our special alkaline water—will change the composition of the corn to something different from its dry, raw state. Remember when we chewed on that uncooked kernel in the precook step (see page 76)? (If you haven't done so yet, there's still time. I'll wait.) How did that taste? Dry, gritty, tough to chew? While maybe nice for some, field corn is not an appealing food in its precooked state. For most humans, it doesn't even constitute *food* yet. Let's help it get there.

Through the boiling/simmering process, the corn is transformed. The hot water alone begins to break down the corn's natural starches and proteins, for example. Absent of cal, this would still make our corn taste much better than how it started (hello, grits, polenta, and cornmeal!), even if still slightly bland (hello, *unbuttered* grits, polenta, and cornmeal!).

Make the corn taste really good

But we're going one step beyond basic edibility with our cal. Like salt or butter, the right amount of cal develops the organoleptic qualities of the corn. It amplifies the corn's flavor, which has an umami-like quality, and also brings the aroma to a whole new level.

As the corn's proteins and carbohydrates are broken down, the corn softens, and, one theory suggests, volatile flavor and aroma compounds are released. The most pronounced of such compounds is 2-aminoacetophenone, which, some researchers believe, is a byproduct of the corn's tryptophan (an amino acid) reacting with the cal. As it happens, 2-aminoacetophenone is found in other delicious foods like grapes and chestnut honey.

In any event, you just wait—a simmering pot of corn in cal water will fill the room with the homey smell of tortillas in no time. By the end of the cooking-with-cal step, the kernel should be tasty enough on its own for you to want to eat a handful and still find yourself craving another bite. Don't feel like you're a good enough cook to pull this off? Relax. The cal and the heated water are going to be doing this work for you, and you're welcome to take all of the credit for it.

Set the mood for nixtamalization

Let's get the birds and the bees of nixtamalization out of the way and demystify this all together as mature adults. Corn meets cal (in a hot tub, no

less). Things get hot. Clothes (in this case the corn's skin, or pericarp) start coming off. Hours later (yes, hours, depending on how long everyone feels comfortable hanging out in tepid cal water), you have nixtamal babies.

One of life's greatest natural wonders, corn nixtamalization is made possible through the union of corn and cal in a hot bath. The hot water is the bridge, the matchmaker, between our two star-crossed ingredients, corn and cal. Scientifically speaking, every chemical reaction requires energy to occur. Nixtamalization is no different. In this case, our cooking heat (i.e., energy source) increases the caustic action of cal, which, in turn, begins to break down the corn for our culinary needs.

As the water is heated and reaches 167°F [75°C], the first signs of this reaction become visible; the water begins to change to a yellow color, which is a result of the corn's natural pigments (e.g., carotenoids, flavonoids, anthocyanins, etc.) leeching into the water. Some of these antioxidant pigments become partially oxidized in this alkaline cooking state, and they are what ultimately drive the complex flavor structure of our finished masa.

HOW TO COOK WITH CAL

So, now that we understand *why* we cook with cal, let's add some color to *how* to cook with cal.

When cooking with cal, even the most bland varieties of corn should develop some more flavor complexity than they contain in their raw states. This is important to know because with too low a water temperature or too short a cooking time, the finished texture will yield a tasteless, gritty finish (i.e., underdeveloped starch); and, with too high a sustained water temperature or too long a cook time, your corn will become mushy and taste mostly of water (i.e., overdeveloped starch, like what happens when you overcook noodles). The following steps will help you cook a perfect kernel every time.

Setup

Starting with the cal, this is one of the few steps in our entire kernel-to-masa process where I actually specify an exact measurement. I recommend measuring out 1 percent of cal to the weight of the corn that you'll be cooking. If you plan to cook 1 lb [455 g] of corn, for example, this means that you'll need ⅙ oz [4.55 g] of cal. In most traditional settings throughout Mexico, this is an "eyeball it" kinda measurement. Abuelas who have been doing this for decades may be adding slightly more or less than this ratio, and I can't stop you from pursuing this route yourself. But 1 percent cal to corn is a foolproof ratio, no matter the regional dish or application you're going for, so there's really no need to complicate this for yourself by winging it.

Starting Corn Weight (lb)	Cal (oz)	Finished Masa Weight (lb)	Finished Tortillas (at 1 oz, pre cook)	Finished Tortillas Weight (lb)
1	0.16	2.2	35	1.5
2	0.32	4.4	70	3
3	0.48	6.6	106	4.5
4	0.64	8.8	141	6
5	0.8	11	176	7.5
6	0.96	13.2	211	9
7	1.12	15.4	246	10.5
8	1.28	17.6	282	12
9	1.44	19.8	317	13.5
10	1.6	22	352	15

RECOGNIZING TOO LITTLE CAL, TOO MUCH CAL, AND WHEN IT'S JUST RIGHT.

Too little cal:

- The corn's color will look a bit watered down and it will taste relatively bland, lacking umami flavor.
- The skins won't easily peel off or gelatinize, and the corn might never become nixtamal. In this case, we won't get a proper masa.

Too much cal:

- The corn will take on a dark yellow tint, which makes blue corn look green, red look brown, white look yellow, and yellow look yellow(er).
- The lovely flavor effect that cal imparts becomes too much of a good thing. You now taste and smell only cal, which can start to smell a lot like bile or cat pee. Yum.
- We're on our way to making masa, albeit a higher pH masa, which may not be what you're going for.

Just right:

- As the corn's pH rises, its color will brighten. This is a sign that the alkali is going to work. The yellows of xanthophylls become more pronounced, the pinks of anthocyanins will darken, and white corn will become slightly golden in tone.
- The aroma of fresh tortillas, tamales, and even ramen (i.e., "alkaline noodles"), which is often made with cal, will begin to fill the room. We're on our way to making excellent masa.

Once you've measured out the cal in a mixing bowl on a scale, add just enough water to it to create a smooth, well-mixed slurry. This makes the cal easier to incorporate evenly into the pot without clumping. (You are also welcome to add the cal directly to the pot after you've added in the water, if you'd like—this is just my personal preference.) For $\frac{1}{6}$ oz [4.55 g] of cal, for example, a half cup should be plenty. I'll then pour the slurry into the pot holding my corn.

Next, I'll fill the pot with enough water to cover the corn by 4 to 6 in [10 to 15 cm], mixing everything together with a wooden spatula. Keep in mind that, if needed, you can always add more water to the pot later on, as water will simultaneously absorb into the corn and evaporate during cooking.

I prefer bringing the cal water and corn to a boil together, rather than boiling the alkaline water first and then adding my corn. Either method is truly fine, so long as you monitor the kernels throughout the process and ensure that they do not overcook. Bringing the corn and alkaline water up to the right temperature merely ensures a consistent temperature climb, whereas adding corn after the water has reached the desired temperature will drop the temperature immediately. Once the mixture comes to a boil, I will then lower the temperature to a nice even simmer, stirring every few minutes.

Before boil/simmer

During boil/simmer

IDEAL CAL-TO-WATER RATIO

If you wish to be more precise with your water measurement, food scientist and Texas A&M faculty member Dr. Helbert Almeida recommends 1 part corn to 3 parts water by weight. You don't want to exceed this ratio because you otherwise risk diluting the effect of the cal.

Why? When reacting with warm water, a large portion of the cal will fail to fully dissolve. These insoluble cal particles remain in suspension, or float, throughout the water. Even with our 1 percent cal to corn ratio, this means that the water is oversaturated with cal. But, make no mistake: This is intentional. We want to create a condition wherein the cal is not only interacting with the corn on the exterior of the kernel; we also want to ensure that there is plenty of remaining cal to spare. That way, when the water eventually enters the corn kernel during the cooking and steeping processes, there is sufficient cal accompanying the water inside. This ensures that the cal breaks down the corn's cell walls from within, readying the starches and proteins for masa making. Without this step, we would produce an underdeveloped masa network structure that is prone to breaking.

Cooking the corn

I'm going to let you in on a secret: There is no hard-and-fast rule for cooking times.

Overachievers, please don't be frustrated by this. You are welcome to create detailed logs of every corn varietal you'll ever work with, their moisture levels, and their starch densities, and create cooking time averages for each one over the rest of your lifetime. Large-scale tortilla factories have been doing so for decades. You're amazing and in the company of masa greatness if you follow in their footsteps.

But really, that's not what this cooking step is about. Here, cooking is more sensory driven; it's all about setting the mood for what happens next (nixtamalization), remember? Besides, cooking times depend on heat sources, all of which range in power

and output. You may be using a gas stove, which functions differently from your neighbor's electric stove, a chef's professional range, or a portable induction burner. So let's break this down along universal lines.

No matter the heat source or exact temperature, I will check on the corn every five minutes, from the start of the boil and throughout the simmer. You can then turn off the heat and initiate the steeping (nixtamalization) process as soon as *both* of the following conditions are met:

1. The skins have loosened to the point where they easily rub off in between your fingers. I mean *easily*. They should also be sticky to touch. If you have to overthink it or work too hard, if you have to scratch the skins off with your fingernail, then let the corn cook for another five minutes and check again.

2. The corn is now tasting like a delicious food. (Generally speaking, though not always, the skins will have loosened before the corn starts to taste really good.) The flavor should have the unmistakable notes of a delicious tortilla or pozole in the making. The corn is tender, but al dente; medium-soft, but still with some resistance to the bite. Imagine the texture of a tender roasted cashew or boiled peanut—that's roughly what you're looking for. If these two conditions are not met after 60 to 75 minutes of cooking, you can assume that the cal is either insufficient in quantity (did you get your ratio right?) or weaker than needed (cal

STARCH GELATINIZATION While we focus primarily on the sensory aspects—or *art*—of cooking with cal, this is not to say that there isn't any science worth considering in this step. Large-scale masa manufacturers refer specifically to the gelatinization point of the corn's starch, which occurs between 131°F and 149°F [55°C and 65°C] (internal temperature), depending on the corn's maturity, to dictate their cooking and steeping times. It is at this gelatinization point that the starch granules become activated for the purpose of creating masa, and heat can thereafter be reduced to initiate steeping.

Of course, starch is only one component of the masa's overall network structure, the entirety of which consists of fats, proteins, gums, etc. With that said, however, the starch gelatinization point is used as the primary index for determining the corn's overall doneness. In other words, when the starch has reached its gelatinization temperature, it is safe to assume that the corn is on track for complete nixtamalization.

can lose its potency over time—see page 39). In either case, you'll want to begin anew for best results.

Once the skins have sufficiently loosened and the corn has bloomed in flavor, it's time to turn off the heat. Keep in mind, however, that even with the heat turned off, the corn will continue to cook as the water temperature slowly lowers over several hours during the nixtamalization/steeping process. This means that you can expect the corn to soften even further beyond the ideal al dente state and potentially into a much softer texture. Don't be surprised by this; expect the corn to cook another 10 to 20 percent, and plan accordingly.

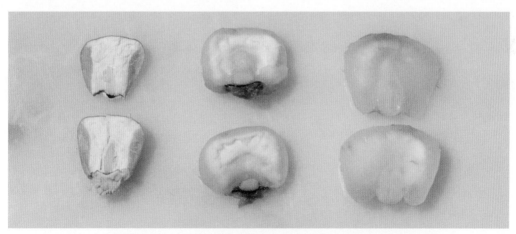

Undercooked kernels *(left)*, **appropriately cooked kernels** *(center)*, **and overcooked kernels** *(right)*.

If you feel like you have taken the corn a little too far before the heat is turned off, or if you like its texture exactly where it is and don't want the corn to cook much further, you can shock the pot with ice. This can be done either directly inside the pot or by submerging the pot into an ice bath. In either case, shocking the pot serves to quickly bring down the temperature. I first saw chef Daniela Soto-Innes use this approach while at Cosme in New York City, which she believed also preserved the color of the corn, much as you'd see with blanching broccoli or asparagus, for example. Keep in mind, however, that the steeping process does benefit from some residual heat (as low as 122°F [50°C]), which optimizes the diffusion of water and cal into the corn kernel, over time.

Note: As the corn cooks, some water will evaporate in the form of steam. Be sure to top up the water level so there's at least 4 in [10 cm] of water above the corn before beginning the steep. This will allow for continued evaporation and kernel absorption of the water, without drying the kernels out in the process.

STEP 3

Nixtamalization

As we covered in the prehistory of masa, nixtamalization is in the vaunted pantheon of mankind's greatest achievements ever, right up there alongside electricity and the wheel. Without it, there is no masa.

Nixtamalization technically encompasses the whole process of cooking and steeping corn in an alkaline solution, but I have isolated it as a standalone steeping step because this is where its alchemy is fully realized.

WHY WE NEED NIXTAMALIZATION

In the transformation of corn into masa, nixtamalization serves a few basic, critical purposes.

Sterilization

This consideration was more dire in ancient times, before humans understood microbial activity and could safely manipulate it. Nixtamalization nevertheless remains an effective way of ensuring the corn is safe for our consumption. Coupled with the high cooking heat, the high pH of the cal (12.4 pH, on average) is enough to destroy most harmful bacteria that could make us sick. In food safety and health department parlance, it's an effective kill step for ensuring the corn is A-rated for human consumption.

Further, the alkalinity of the cal is effective in slightly curbing the masa's

perishability. For this reason, some folks tend to cook with more than 1 percent cal to corn; it can increase the pH and effectively extend the shelf life of your masa by a few hours and your finished tortilla by a few days.

Activation

Contrary to what any wellness nay-sayer might suggest, field corn can be incredibly nutritious, provided that it goes through nixtamalization. Most notably, corn is high in vitamin B_3, or niacin, a key nutrient for human survival. Without nixtamalization, however, this niacin exists in a bound form that cannot be absorbed by the human body. It requires the alkaline treatment to free itself from its chemical bond to other molecules, which in turn activates its bioavailability in each kernel. Further, nixtamalization allows otherwise insoluble fibers in corn to become soluble for human consumption.

Sure, without nixtamalization, it's true that corn would not be the "superfood" it is otherwise capable of becoming. But we're nixtamalizing, so indulge yourself.

Fortification

As an active ingredient in nixtamalization, the cal gives our now-activated corn a healthy boost of calcium. More wellness for you.

Gelatinization and emulsification

Because corn does not contain gluten—that protein found in wheat that helps dough easily stretch without breaking—we basically have to hotwire its skins to achieve a similar function for our masa. Nixtamalization disrupts the continuity of the corn's membranes, which opens up its cell walls, releasing everything inside and exposing the cell contents to each other. This is critical in order for all of the ground corn's components to ultimately bind into a cohesive mass and network structure. Simply put, without nixtamalization, there is no tortilla—at least not the kind that we are all craving by now.

Nixtamalization breaks down the pectin and hemicellulose within the dense cell walls of the corn, causing the entire kernel to dramatically soften in composition. In the process, the corn's pericarp, or outer skin/hull, which also contains pectin, converts into a gelatinous* state and separates from the kernel. The now-gummy traces of pectin within the corn's loosened pericarp and remaining kernel are what will soon partly help make our emulsified, cohesive masa possible, through a process called cross-linking.

In cross-linking, pectin molecules latch onto one another with the aid of calcium. Calcium, as we know, is in abundant supply within calcium hydroxide (cal); it therefore becomes a bridge that connects the pectin's molecular chains to one another, once the nixtamalized corn is ground into a dough. As these chains are eventually kneaded and mixed together in the masa mixing stage (see page 98), they further bind to one another by way of the calcium, in the process creating an elastic web of pectin throughout

---

* According to Harold McGee, *gelatinization* is a bit of a misnomer because the pericarp is not technically rendered into gelatin, but he too concedes that the word helpfully describes the effect and resulting consistency of nixtamalization.

the masa. Not only does this web help give the masa structure, it also gives it elasticity. As when used in jams and jellies, the pectin retains water and sets it into a gel. The result is a moist masa that can be worked into a number of shapes and forms without falling apart.

Remember when we tested the corn kernels between our fingertips, right when the corn started to taste delicious (see page 82)? Their skins were kind of sticky then. After nixtamalization is complete, they're really sticky, almost verging on slimy and pulp-like. Normally, I'd understand if you were a bit turned off by the texture, but this is actually what we want and need to keep the corn's starches from falling apart later on in a tortilla. And a little bit of those skins will go a long way to help keep our masa pliable.

When it comes to nixtamalization, there's really nothing for you to actively *do*. The corn steeps in the warm alkaline water; science just sort of happens to the corn, and it's ready for masa before we know it. Notwithstanding that, it's important to know that some variables remain in your control, which you may manipulate according to your preference.

STEEP TIME

Corn kernels are quite impermeable. For this reason, the warm water, along with the insoluble cal particles suspended in it, needs time to attack the corn's cell walls and penetrate its cells to reach the proteins and starch within the interior. Steeping is necessary to fully realize the nixtamalization process, and there is no substitute

for time. A majority of the visual transformation of the corn takes place within the first hour of the steep. The nixtamalization process benefits from some residual heat, as low as 122°F [50°C], to effectively diffuse water and cal into the corn kernels.

Total steep time will vary, depending on whom you ask and the size of their production. For some industrial tortillerias, for example, steep times can be as short as 3 to 4 hours. This abbreviated steep is possible because of the high density of corn being cooked at a time. Barring an ice bath (see page 84), you'll recall that steeping is a gradual continuation of the cooking process. And, when cooking one thousand-pound batches and more, the heat retention is much greater than, say, a pot of five pounds of corn at home. This results in a higher sustained temperature during the steep, which not only accelerates the diffusion of the water and cal into the corn, but also the corn's cook. Translation: nixtamalization is sped up. Any additional steeping at this scale may result in overcooked corn.

For those home cooks looking for a solid prescribed range that won't disappoint, I'd recommend steeping for 6 to 12 hours (i.e., overnight) at ambient temperature. This is enough time to ensure that the job gets done but not so much time that the nixtamal ferments or becomes a fossil. Note: If you do let it go for a bit longer, it should still be okay. I'll sometimes get busy doing something else, for example, and take it to 24 hours or so, which has always been fine.

WOOD ASH NIXTAMAL

While this might appear especially ancient, wood ash nixtamal can still be found throughout much of the masa foodway today. In Oaxaca, for example, some artisans use wood ash specifically for nixtamalizing corn for tlayudas and pozole. Personally, I first learned about this process from Craig Deihl, a southern chef who prepared hominy (a.k.a. pozole, see page 145) with wood ash when he led the kitchen at the now-closed Cypress restaurant in Charleston, South Carolina.

Although I don't always have spare wood ash lying around my "homestead" (note: As of writing this, I currently live in a small Los Angeles apartment with a fake gas fireplace and a strict HOA), I absolutely love this way of preparing nixtamal. For starters, the flavor of the finished nixtamal and masa has a distinctly smoky, campfire essence, which I find especially complements roasted vegetables and grilled fish, though any pairing works, really. There's also something rustic, elemental, and primordial to me about this method that I find quite romantic.

Clocking in at a pH of about 11.3, wood ash is more than ten times *less* caustic than cal, which is approximately 12.4 pH. The pH scale is logarithmic, which means that a difference of one integer value (e.g., 12 to 11) changes the concentration by a factor of 10. This means that it takes a bit more ash to get the job done than cal.

For this reason, we'll use a ratio of 1 part ash to 1 part corn, by volume. For example, one cup of corn will require one cup of ash to get the job done. (By weight, this ratio works out to be about 1 part ash to 2 parts corn, depending on the size and density of the corn kernels used.)

Because ash has common applications beyond nixtamalization, including soap making and as a soil amendment, it is easy to find sifted wood ash online, if you don't happen to have any on hand. Alternatively, you can hit up your nearest wood-fired restaurant for some, as it's usually thrown out at the end of an evening's service. (Special thanks to chef Juan and Max at Gjelina restaurant for Masienda's local ash hookup.)

Preparation

First things first, make sure your ash has sufficiently cooled and that no embers remain. (I may or may not have scorched the carpet of my car on at least one occasion when transporting ash that had not fully cooled.) This can take up to two or three days, depending on how compacted and insulated the ash is.

Once cool, you'll want to sift the ash with a fine-mesh sieve. Lumps of charcoal, partially-cooked wood, etc. should be separated and discarded, so that only an evenly-sifted ash remains for use.

You may then place the ash directly in a nonreactive pot containing corn and water, as you would with cal. However, I find it best to first prepare a strained ash solution, what I call a "quick lye," instead. Otherwise, the ash can weigh down the corn, causing it to scorch at the bottom of the pot; it can also be quite difficult to clean the corn afterward without discarding all of the skins or clogging your drain with wet ash.

To create the ash solution, place your ash in a nonreactive pot and cover with water. I recommend 4 parts water to 1 part ash, by volume.

Bring the water and ash to a boil and reduce to a simmer. Cook for 15 minutes and let rest for another 30. The ash should settle to the bottom of the pot, while the liquid sitting above it will have intensified in its pH to about 12. If you were to continue to let the solution rest for several days, the resulting liquid at the top could develop into lye (depending, among other factors, on how hard your tap water is) which is around pH 13, and nearly ten times more caustic than cal.

Carefully strain the solution with a fine-mesh sieve, taking care to not agitate the ash, which will muddy the solution. Most importantly, remember that lye and cal are highly caustic and can cause irritation and/or skin burns, so exercise healthy caution. Don't worry about leaving some of the solution behind in the process. You may discard any remaining liquid down the drain (it will give your plumbing a good cleanse) and compost or dispose of the wood ash in the garbage.

You may then add the quick lye directly to your nonreactive pot with which you'll cook your corn. Then, follow steps for either Table Tortilla Masa (page 114), Frying Tortilla Masa (page 132), or Pozole (page 145).

ALKALINITY

Central to nixtamalization is the use of an alkaline (that is, pH basic) solution to break down the cell walls of the corn. The level of alkalinity is most commonly manipulated with cal, though other alkaline substances—from wood ash to mussel shells—have also been traditionally used for the same purpose.

While corn's relationship with nixtamalization is unique, other grains and vegetables, from wheat berries to pumpkin, may also be nixtamalized with varying results.

Not only does cal facilitate nixtamalization, it's also used to manipulate shelf life. You'll remember that cal works on the exterior of the corn and, through gradual diffusion during the steeping process, interacts with the interior of the corn as well. This ultimately increases the pH of the corn itself, among other effects.

The higher the cal ratio, the more basic (pH) the corn becomes, producing an incrementally more shelf-stable masa and tortilla. (See page 253 for a handy pH chart).

For example, a high-pH tortilla, at 11 pH, with no additional preservatives, might last for one to two weeks at ambient temperatures before molding, compared to a neutral 7 pH tortilla that may last one to two days, at most. Cal is such a widely used "natural" form of preservation that additional amounts of it are often added directly to a finished masa, before it's sheeted or formed into tortillas.

As we covered in the Cooking with Cal step (page 77), remember that too much cal can develop a highly pungent aroma and flavor in a tortilla, serving to mask the flavor of the corn itself. Likewise, the higher the ratio of cal to corn in the steeping process, the more its yellow coloring will tint the pigments of the finished product.

Given how many factors alkalinity affects—including masa workability, color, aroma, shelf life, and flavor—alkalinity control is a masa-making lever with big implications.

While alkalinity is primarily controlled in the Cooking with Cal step (page 77), it is important to reiterate its impact on the overall nixtamalization process. Again, as a general rule of thumb, I suggest beginning with a 1 percent ratio of cal to the total weight of corn. And, so long as the pericarp is sufficiently broken down during nixtamalization, you may choose to add additional cal to the finished masa later on to manipulate flavor, color, and shelf life (it's an oft-used trick of the tortilleria trade).

Regardless of how you choose to manipulate these variables, by the end of the nixtamalization process, our corn is no longer just corn.

It is now irreversibly, and henceforth called, *nixtamal*.

that is, the estimated percentage of skins washed off and/or discarded before the milling process. I recommend starting with a 50 percent wash-off percentage, and working your way up or down according to preference and varietal, moving forward, once you have established a baseline look and feel.

PRO TIP: Because it can be tough to get an accurate sense of just how much you are washing off, it is sometimes helpful to measure out by dividing your nixtamal according to your desired wash-off percentage. If, for example, I wanted to get a 50 percent wash-off, I would weigh or eyeball half of my nixtamal and wash that half to the point where no skins remained. I'd then mix the remaining half together with my washed corn for an even blend.

STEP 4

Nixtamal Rinsing

Despite being a relatively short step in the kernel-to-masa process, rinsing your nixtamal is nevertheless an important one.

The pericarp contains much of the corn's natural gums, a key binding agent that will serve our masa well. Especially if your goal is a pliable table tortilla with good elasticity, you'll want to control just how much or how little of the skins accompany your nixtamal for grinding.

The rinsing process will typically involve some degree of agitation of the nixtamal, either before or after you discard the alkaline water. Agitation, or briskly stirring, serves to further loosen and separate the skins from the kernels.

The extent to which you agitate and rinse the nixtamal will ultimately impact your wash-off percentage—

While the network structure of masa is composed of the same essential elements (e.g., starch, gums, oil, etc.), each corn varietal looks different insofar as its ratios or proportions of each of those elements. Some corn may have a higher oil content than others, less or more protein, etc. This means that some varietals might benefit from more skins than others. While there is no hard-and-fast rule for wash-off percentages, a 50 percent wash-off will help achieve consistency across all corn varietals used for masa.

So why rinse the corn or wash off any of the skins at all?

To control the texture

Assuming 100 percent of the nixtamalized pericarp were to make its way into the resulting masa, you would likely end up with a very elastic, albeit gummy finish in your final application. And in a fried tortilla, for example, that result will be an even tougher version of itself that could verge on being difficult to chew. However, this might be a good approach for recipe-style tortillas or chips that are eventually covered and cooked in sauces at high temperatures, like chilaquiles, as the structure of the tortilla will hold together far better in such applications. A higher proportion of skins in the nixtamal is also an effective way to avoid the need to introduce gums or stabilizers like guar or xanthan gum, especially for tortillas that might not be consumed fresh within the same day (as is the case with many retail tortillas).

Alternatively, fewer skins can translate to an easier bite overall, which can be a more desirable texture for your everyday table tortilla.

In any event, it's a lever that you can add to your repertoire for manipulating the texture and overall workability of the finished masa.

To offset the cal

Our nixtamal is coming from a highly alkaline bath, which carries its own distinct flavor, color, and pH. The rinse is therefore an opportunity to adjust these three factors according to your desired preference.

Nixtamal Grinding

At long last, we're ready to make masa. For the purposes of this section, I will go into relative depth on the use of an electric basalt stone molino (mill) for grinding nixtamal. The reason is twofold: First, a molino is the most efficient tool to achieve a wide range of masa textures, especially those finer grinds that we're used to seeing in a classic table tortilla (page 119). As Harold McGee writes, "stone grinding cuts the kernels, mashes them, and kneads the mass, mixing together starch, protein, oils, emulsifiers, and cell wall materials, and the lime's molecule-bridging calcium." You'd be hard pressed to compete with that level of utility in any other tool.

Second, more often than not, the molino is a tool that comes with few, if any operating instructions. Thus, given the rising interest in the subject and the recent availability of more economical, compact molinos like the Molinito (see page 252 for additional information), it felt appropriate to provide some instruction (finally!) on how to use one.

If you don't have a molino, however, don't worry! I will cover the basics of nixtamal grinding with both a hand mill and a food processor. Believe it or not, these alternatives will be much more straightforward (not to mention less expensive) than operating a molino, even if it takes just a bit more elbow grease or time to get the job done.

GRINDING WITH A MOLINO

Typically a one-person job, this is perhaps the most technically involved step in the kernel-to-masa cycle. It is a coordinated dance of 1), calibrating the stone settings, 2), adjusting the water trickle into the hopper, 3), steadily feeding the molino's auger with nixtamal, and 4), monitoring the resulting masa quality. Suffice it to say, grinding this way can be a rather intimidating process at first. Given that the machine is doing the lion's share of the work, however, let's break down the variables into manageable parts within our immediate control.

STONE SETTING

The electric molino consists of two stones with their carved surfaces facing one another.

One stone, usually slightly larger, will be locked in place so that it remains steady and stationary, while the other stone moves in a spinning motion propelled by the molino's motor. The stones can be set widely apart from one another or adjusted until they are tightly pressed together. As you can probably deduce, the closer the stones are to one another, the finer the grind; the farther they are from one another, the coarser the grind. Too far in either direction and you'll either burn out your motor, which occurs when the motor runs too long while the stones are locked in with each other, or have entire kernels of nixtamal fall through the gap between the stones, completely untouched.

When first dialing in to your desired grind, tighten the stone calibration screw until you start to feel resistance (that is, the stones begin to touch), and then loosen the screw with about a half turn in the opposite direction. From there you can gradually tighten to the setting that produces your desired masa finish (see page 96, "Assessing your masa quality").

In the early stages of becoming accustomed to a stone mill, many cooks err on the side of leaving too much space between the stones, producing a coarser grind than they'd like. It's understandable: Between the cost of the equipment and the screeching noises a mill can make, bringing the stones so close together can be scary at first. But, take my word for it, this is something you'll grow more comfortable with over time. If something seems off, don't panic. Turn off the mill and start over. Keep doing this until you get the hang of it. Assuming you aren't letting the machine run inefficiently for several minutes at a time, the worst that can happen is a faster wearing down of your stones, which can always be resharpened or replaced entirely.

WATER TRICKLE

A water trickle is used for lubricating the nixtamal so that it passes smoothly into the molino's auger (called a *gusano*, or "worm," in tortilleria lingo) and through the stones. Further, when the stones are pressed closely to one another (as is the case for grinding nixtamal into a masa for table tortillas), they create a great deal of friction, which generates a lot of heat. Managing the water trickle just right ensures that the stones don't overheat. To this end, it is also helpful to soak the stones in water for 5 to 10 minutes before beginning your grind.

Many large molinos include either a water tank with a spigot positioned above the hopper or a custom plumbing line that connects to a trickle faucet above the hopper. If your molino does not have a built-in trickle, you can easily create one by poking a hole (about ⅛ in [3 mm] wide) into the top of a plastic water bottle (see photo to right).

As you adjust the water, keep in mind that too much water will translate to a wetter, tackier masa. A very thin stream of water should suffice (cut or increase the flow intermittently, as necessary, to adjust for either increased friction/heat or too tacky a finished masa). The ideal is a slow flow. Think of your bathroom sink faucet on the lowest setting just before shutting off. As we'll cover in the next section, we can always adjust for moisture in the masa mixing stage. For now, we're thinking of the water trickle solely in terms of facilitating the milling process.

FEEDING THE AUGER

The first time I used a molino, I filled the hopper with as much nixtamal as it could hold before turning on the molino. My thinking was that loading the nixtamal would be one less thing I'd have to worry about during the milling process, which would free me up to focus on the water trickle and the masa quality coming out of the stones.

But within a minute of my starting the mill, the stones started to overheat, and a screeching sound began to crescendo throughout the room. Then . . . the smell of burning.

I remembered that overheating could be related to a lack of nixtamal lubrication, so I turned up the water trickle. No luck. The noise and smell continued, and within 30 seconds I noticed that the only thing passing through the stones was water, which had begun to form an unappetizing-looking puddle in the masa collection chamber.

My rookie mistake? Overloading the hopper, which caused the nixtamal to compact and stay in place rather than flow freely through the auger. After letting the molino cool down for a moment and drying down the masa collection chamber, I removed enough of the nixtamal so that I could now easily see the auger in action. Flipping the power switch back on, it was clear that the auger occasionally needed assistance to ensure a constant pull of nixtamal from the hopper.

Takeaway 1: Load the hopper with only a handful or two of nixtamal at a time, depending on the size of your molino. For the Molinito (pictured on page 95), we recommend feeding a pinch (10 to 15 kernels) at a time.

Takeaway 2: Use a wooden or plastic spatula to constantly move the nixtamal around in the hopper so that the auger is always pulling nixtamal through the stones. It helps guide the nixtamal in the same direction that the auger itself is moving.

ASSESSING YOUR MASA QUALITY

As you feed the auger and monitor your water trickle, do a check on the resulting masa. Healthy masa should shoot off the stones like fast-moving snowflakes. To get a sense of texture, safely place your hand (face up) about 3 in [7.5 cm] below the stones. After 3 to 5 seconds, a small bit of masa will collect in your hand. Roll the masa into a ball. Rub the ball between your fingertips and check for:

Texture
Do you feel a lot of coarse particles in the masa? If so, perhaps you can stand to tighten the stones further (especially if going for a masa for table tortillas). If you detect gummy bits or rubbery chunks, it's best to turn off the machine and lower the stone friction by either loosening the stones or increasing the water trickle to prevent overheating. The ideal texture is moist but not sticky, pliable but not gummy. We'll get into more specific texture recommendations in our Masa Recipes (page 105).

Aroma
The masa should smell fragrant, like steaming, nixtamalized corn. If you detect a burning machinery smell, turn off the machine and take a minute to reset your stones and trickle.

Color
The masa should be a slightly lighter tint than the nixtamal itself. If it's flecked with dark gray bits, you'll likely also see gummier bits of masa coming out. Be sure to remove these (as their flavor and texture are generally unpleasant) and adjust your stones and trickle accordingly.

GRINDING WITH A HAND MILL

A hand-cranked corn mill is perhaps the simplest way to grind nixtamal into masa. And, contrary to any early doubts I ever had about achieving masa for a puffable table tortilla with one, a hand mill is absolutely capable of getting you there.

To begin, tighten the metal plates as much as they will allow, and then open them up in the opposite (loose) direction with a half turn. Next, feed a small scoop of nixtamal into the hopper. Give the mill a few cranks so that nixtamal starts moving through the auger and the grinding plates. This should produce coarse nixtamal shavings, which will help coat the metal plates. Then, tighten the grinding plates to their tightest position and crank away. A well-hydrated nixtamal will help achieve the desired masa consistency on the first pass.

While additional passes through the mill can help produce an even finer masa, it can be difficult for the ground masa to travel through the mill for a second or third time. Provided you incorporate a little trickle of water as you mill your nixtamal, you should get puffable masa after the first pass.

GRINDING WITH A FOOD PROCESSOR

The food processor is perhaps the most convenient grinding tool (though it technically cuts the nixtamal, not grinds), as many cooks already have one in their home kitchen.

To begin, fill the food processor about halfway with nixtamal and pulse for one to two minutes until it becomes coarsely ground. You may need to break this process up into smaller batches, depending on the size of your food processor and/or nixtamal batch. Remove the lid and scrape the sides of the container with a spatula. After replacing the lid, add a splash of water and then turn the food processor back on. With the blades running, slowly add water until a cohesive paste

begins to form. Continue until the paste becomes smooth (5 to 7 minutes), pausing, as necessary, to scrape the sides of the container.

Once ground, the masa will be quite wet and sticky. To get the masa to a workable state, you may then choose to do one of two things.

1. Incorporate a bit of dry masa harina into the wet masa, thereby reducing the overall moisture. This can be done manually (kneading by hand) or in a stand mixer with a dough hook or paddle attachment.

2. Dry the wet masa in the oven. Preheat the oven to 200°F [95°C]. Transfer the wet masa from the food processor to a rimmed baking sheet. Spread the masa evenly across the surface and bake until the top yields a slight crust; it should be noticeably drier and no longer sticky, 15 to 20 minutes, depending on how thick and

wet the layer of masa is. You may need to break this process up into smaller batches, depending on the size of your baking sheet and/or masa batch.

In either case, the ideal finished texture should be moist but not sticky, pliable but not gummy.

STEP 6

Masa Mixing

As we touched on earlier, the electric molino is a super tool that does a lot more than just break down nixtamal. As perfect as its resulting masa may seem, it is not quite ready for shaping until it's been properly mixed together, whether by hand or in a stand mixer with a dough hook attachment. The same goes for masa made with either a hand-cranked mill or a food processor.

For reference, most tortillerias average about 5 minutes for mechanically mixing each batch of masa before being pressed into tortillas. I'd be sure to get in at least 2 minutes of mixing. If you should happen to mix for longer, don't worry about overworking the masa; its absence of gluten will prevent a gummy mass from forming.

We mix the masa for these reasons:

Texture consistency
Think of how we were constantly adjusting water trickle, stone calibration, and so on, and how each adjustment yields a slightly different masa texture. The goal is to achieve a single cohesive mixture with uniform texture so that each tortilla—or whichever masa shape you are making—from that batch is consistent with the rest.

Seasoning, color, and flavor control
Salt, chile paste, cilantro juice, beet juice, nopal—this is your chance to adjust seasoning, color (see page 102), and flavor, if you so desire. A little bit of salt (0.25 percent is my own personal preference) goes a long way to teasing out the nixtamal's flavors, but it's certainly not necessary to add. On a humbler note: In times of scarcity, whether due to drought or other inclement weather, milpa farmers will mix in other ingredients, like herbs, quelites (wild-foraged greens), or other cheap and accessible ingredients in order to stretch the masa as far as possible.

Moisture control

Table tortillas, for example, need a good amount of moisture to generate enough steam to puff, or soufflé, later on. To achieve this consistency, the masa should be just wet enough. Too much water will make it tacky, which looks like masa sticking in large, uneven chunks to your fingers. You can use the mixing step to slowly incorporate enough water to reach the ideal state.

By contrast, if you produced a tacky masa by either overcooking your nixtamal or going heavy on the water trickle during the milling process, mixing can serve as a corrective step. Either let the masa dry out over several minutes (some folks direct a fan onto the masa or refrigerate it for 30 minutes to an hour) or slowly add dry masa flour to the wet masa until you reach the optimal moisture and texture.

Alkalinity control

Many tortillerias will have a pH meter somewhere in-house, used to control for the alkalinity in each batch. This is not necessary when making masa at home; however, if you are curious about tracking this, it is a cheap investment. At this point in the mixing stage, some tortillerxs choose to add cal directly to the masa, if a higher pH is desired. If you choose to do the same, note that the proportions of cal to pH level are not exactly evenly correlated. You'll do best to slowly incorporate small (0.10 percent) increments of cal at a time until you reach your desired pH. You may conversely choose to lower the pH by diluting the wet masa with masa harina and/or other dry, lower pH ingredients.

Additives

Many tortillerias choose to add preservatives, gums, and/or stabilizers to their masa. In some cases, their conveyor ovens may have been designed for Maseca, in which case a little extra binding agent (for example, xanthan, cellulose, or guar gums, and even additional cal) is needed to ensure that the masa rolls onto the conveyor properly. In other cases, preservatives are added to manage microbial stability between production and distribution and, ultimately, consumption, which may be months from production. While you may approach these additives however you see fit, keep in mind that they do change the flavor of the masa that you've just spent hours making. Especially in the case of preservatives like propionic acid, the taste is—you guessed it—highly acidic. These acids also have a bleaching effect on color.

Right: **Each masa ball reflects a different pH level, from acidic to neutral to basic. The acidic (purple) sample was achieved by adding lemon juice (~3 pH) to neutral blue masa. The basic (green) sample was achieved by adding cal (12.4 pH) to neutral blue masa. The neutral blue sample was the control at 7 pH.**

BASIC

NEUTRAL

ACIDIC

DYEING MASA

Long-time Masienda partner, friend, and collaborator, chef Christine Rivera is known for her playful approach to masa colors. Rivera's masa program uses a base of blue and white heirloom corns, while achieving a rainbow of additional colors and flavors from ingredients like carrot (for orange), beet (for pink), purple cabbage (for purple), hoja santa (for green), and squid ink (for black), to name a few. She'll even pair different batch colors of masa within a single tortilla, creating a highly photogenic tie-dye and/or rainbow effect. While juices of each ingredient can be used, they may make the masa moister than you may desire. For this reason, Christine is partial to dehydrating her "dye" ingredients (with the exception of squid ink), pulverizing them into powders, and adding them accordingly to her masa during the mixing stage.

Masa

Recipes

While the preparation of masa itself has yet to receive much focused, long-form literary attention, its culinary applications have been covered prolifically over the years. Most notably, the works of Diana Kennedy, Patricia Quintana, Rick Bayless, and Ricardo Muñoz Zurita have done much to document some of the more popular dishes involving masa in Mexico, specifically. Diana Kennedy, for example, wrote a comprehensive collection of regional tamales recipes in her books, *The Cuisines of Mexico* and *The Art of Mexican Cooking*, which deserve due respect. Suffice it to say, a wholly "new" recipe on tamales will not be included in this section. What will be included, however is a selection of traditional recipes and modern masa marvels intended to achieve a few goals in the name of masa.

CONTEXTUALIZING MASA

My first goal was to contextualize the kinds of masa we find ourselves using, knowingly or unknowingly, from dish to dish. All masa is not created equal, and the first part of the chapter is meant to lay the recommended foundation upon which the subsequent, breakout dishes are built.

TRADITIONAL APPLICATIONS

Second, I have organized, from as many resources, cultures, and personal experiences as possible, the vast world of masa's culinary applications into some semblance of a unified body, each dish being included according to its relationship to masa, regardless of origin. The research to do so involved pulling from disparate sources—personal experience, cookbooks, YouTube videos, and so on—to compile a dedicated record of masa uses. To be clear, these are not *my* recipes; in fact, they do not belong to any one person or culture, necessarily. I merely put into words the traditions that I have observed in the course of my work with masa to date.

Further, while Mexico boasts a wealth of masa wisdom, this is not a recipe chapter on Mexican foods alone. I have done my best to reflect the roots that inspire each recipe and adapt their nuanced formulas to a cohesive approach, but they by no means constitute a *definitive* approach. Masa exists in so many cultures in the world today that it felt limiting to restrict the selection to Mexican applications alone. The Masa Shapes dossier (page 150) is a reflection of this wonderful diversity we find within the masa pantheon, as it were.

MODERN MASA EXPLORATIONS

Finally, this chapter is intended to start a conversation about how masa is used in our daily lives. If I have learned anything about masa, it's that it is not static. While the masa classics are meant to be cataloged, studied, and prepared with gusto, so too should they be adapted, playfully referenced, and modified. With any luck, the small collection of modern masa marvels that I have assembled here will accomplish just that. Miles Davis couldn't limit his scope of jazz to *Kind of Blue*, and masa couldn't be kept from growing into the international, multigenerational phenomenon that it has become.

EXPERIMENTING WITH MASA

With these goals in mind, there are two ways to have fun with these recipes. One is to build your masa base and, with your newfound skill, apply it to some of your favorite cookbooks, online resources, or inherited recipes that call for masa. The other is to build your masa base and begin playing with some of the foods you already have in your repertoire, refrigerator, or pantry that may have previously had little in common with masa. Leftover chicken salad? Put it on a sope (page 199). Unsure what to do with those canned beans you've had in your pantry for months? Whip up some memelas (page 181), topped with whatever cheese or hot sauce you've got to your name, or boil some chochoyotes (page 165) and throw them in there. Masa is an instrumental food with infinite potential. Get to know it and use it everywhere. This guide will show you how.

Note: Cooking times should be considered approximate, given wide-ranging differences in comals, utensils, elevation, and so on.

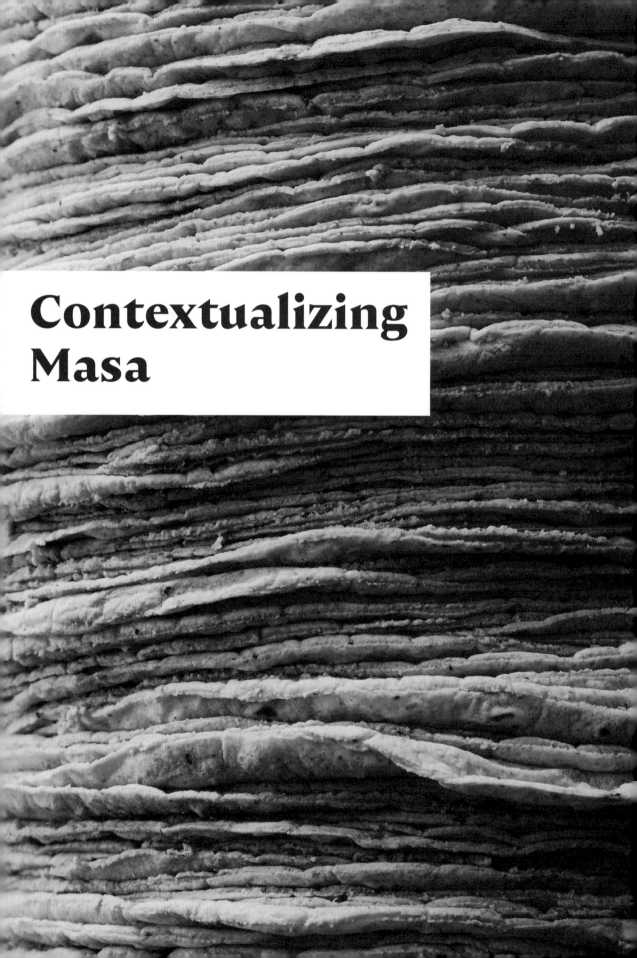

Contextualizing Masa

Tortillas:
An Introduction

I wish I had a more original analogy, but the humble tortilla is much like a proverbial iceberg. On its face, it seems simple enough; however, its essential composition of corn, water, and cal belies just how much culinary nuance there is beneath the surface.

No one I have ever known appreciates this paradox better than the Lopez family of the El Milagro tortilla dynasty.

I first met Jesse Lopez, one of the thirteen total Lopez siblings (seven of whom are still involved with El Milagro), in 2015, under the auspices of a retail tortilla line that Masienda was considering launching with a major grocer. Without Masienda's own tortilleria, we'd needed a co-packer with whom to collaborate on transforming Masienda corn into a retail-ready tortilla.

Jesse and I met at El Milagro's 36th Street location in Chicago's Archer Heights neighborhood, one of five forty-thousand-plus-square-foot production facilities within a two-mile radius of one another.

Up until that point, the tortillerias I had visited in the United States and Mexico were little more than open-air garage spaces with a small cooking tank or two, a scrappy molino with a rusted frame, and a squeaky, single-row tortilla oven that was operated by, at most, two people at a time. In fact, most of the so-called factories I'd seen were really just that: garages.

Sure, they were a bit informal, I reasoned, but they'd always gotten the job done. Even if they didn't exactly use measurements or recipes per se, each had a signature style for their tortilla, which—especially when eaten piping hot, right off the line—was almost impossible to dislike. I saw their buildings' overall roughness around the edges as part of their charm and authenticity.

But we needed a more "polished" facility to manage the output of a retailer. So here I was, cautiously optimistic, in one of the most significant masa cities in all the world.

As I approached El Milagro in a taxi, even from several blocks away I could immediately sense the massive scale at which they operated. There were dozens of El Milagro delivery trucks parked in a separate lot nearby, and a queue of eighteen-wheelers stretched alongside the entire expanse of the entrance. It seemed like all of the semis that I'd ever seen on the highway—whose logos stood out on every road trip I'd ever taken, but whose contents were always a mystery—had converged on this concrete-faced, nondescript warehouse.

After I signed in with security and donned a fresh single-use hairnet, Jesse started the tour. "This is our laboratory," he said, pointing to a two-hundred-square-foot room. There were a handful of staff moving productively throughout the room, pipetting samples onto slides and recording notes into handwritten logs. "Every single one of our facilities has one of these."

What on earth could there be to test? I thought to myself. A tortilla is either good or bad, delicious or not. "You said we were meeting at a tortilleria, not a science lab!" I said awkwardly, if not a bit incredulously, to Jesse.

"We'll get there; don't worry" he said with a smile, leading me past their employee cafeteria to our left.

My early skepticism about the buttoned-up manufacturing experience had now given way to full-on disappointment. I couldn't possibly be romanced by whatever corporate, behemoth vision of a tortilleria this might be. It was at complete odds with the humble, wood-fired kitchens in Oaxaca that had inspired tortilla nirvana within me at the very start of my masa journey; this place more closely resembled a scene from *E.T.* than a masa artisan's soulful workshop.

But any misgivings I had about its appearance or authenticity quickly disappeared as we finally reached the threshold of El Milagro's production floor.

Inside, it was like the engine room aboard an aircraft carrier, only a brighter, more expansive, and immaculately clean food-grade version. Directly in front of me was an enormous stainless steel tortilla line that must have stretched for at least a hundred feet, with as many as thirty people working the room, end to end.

Jesse showed me into an adjacent space that contained several cooking tanks raised about 14 ft [4 m] off the ground. Each tank was filled with an excess of 2,000 lb [900 kg] of corn at various stages in the cooking and nixtamalization cycles. He directed me to look above, where he pointed out a series of elaborate pipes with openings positioned above every tank. These were connected to a giant silo system outside that could store up to 125,000 lb [56,700 kg], or two-and-a-half truckloads, of corn at a time.

I caught my jaw from dropping clean off my face before asking how regularly they'd refill the silos per month. Or per year?

Five, sometimes six a *week*. Jesse replied. For one "small" plant alone. All for millions of corn tortillas made the traditional way.

And this plant wasn't even fully dedicated to corn tortillas! As he showed me the balance of the building, Jesse explained that they produced a very specific set of corn tortilla recipes at this location and used the remainder of the space for a handful of flour tortilla recipes and special one-offs.

The diversity of their offerings for this simple staple was absolutely astonishing. Each approach had a specific purpose, whether its end use was for tacos, chips, frying, steaming, baking, spending long periods of time on a retail shelf, no time at all on a retail shelf—the list went on and on.

Jesse proudly shared that El Milagro had a collection of more than one hundred different recipes for the common tortilla. They not only used varying ratios of ingredients—or additives, as requested by customers, in certain cases—for each recipe, but they also had an arsenal of volcanic stone sets for each milling occasion. Each set weighed between 100 to 150 lb [45 to 68 kg], he explained, and bore unique patterns that achieved exacting masa textures.

I noticed that the stones' patterns all faced inward toward one another, hidden from view, and stopped Jesse before moving to the next area of the tour. "May I see an example of the patterns you're talking about?"

Jesse threw his head back and laughed. He said he'd be happy to, but that he'd have to promptly kill me afterward. At the time, no one but the immediate Lopez family members were allowed to even look at the stones in any detail, let alone sharpen them. For almost seventy years, the patterns had been considered their family's highly classified intellectual property. And for their part, at least, the Lopez family seemed intent on keeping it that way.

As the tour wound down, we went to the office area to get down to business matters. Jesse gathered a handful of packs from several recipes they'd produced that morning and fanned them out across their conference room table like a deck of Pantone swatches.

"So, Jorge, what kind of tortilla are you thinking you'd like us to make?"

It reminded me of the time I went to Sherwin-Williams and asked the store clerk for "white paint" (who knew that there were some fifty shades of color between "Marshmallow" and "Egret White"?). What's more, when it came to our ingredient choice, we hadn't even broached the fact that there were another twenty-five heirloom varieties of corn to consider for the recipe.

The possibilities were dizzying.

Sensing an existential crisis in the making, Jesse narrowed things down to simpler terms, albeit they were foreign to me at the time.

"OK, OK, let's start with the basics— do you want a *table* tortilla or a *frying* tortilla?"

TABLE TORTILLAS VERSUS FRYING TORTILLAS

I learned that day that, despite the many volumes of corn tortilla recipes in active rotation at El Milagro, the company, along with other old-school tortillerias across the country, essentially classified all of their formulations according to a simple, binary system.

On one end of the spectrum, you have table tortillas. These are the kind of tortillas that we almost universally envision when we think of a corn tortilla. They are soft, pliable, and ready to be enjoyed immediately. As the name suggests, table tortillas are the ones you'll find passed around the table at mealtime. Mexicans often joke that they can't start a meal until tortillas are on the table; these are the kind they're referring to. They're used as edible utensils. In short, they make the meal.

Table tortillas are shared not only in this capacity, but also in the quintessential "soft-shell" taco

format, though the lines can start to get blurred right around here. Their calling cards are a fine grind and high moisture, which also happen to be key factors in coaxing what is perhaps the table tortilla's most enchanting and sought-after quality: the puff. (We'll get to that on page 126, I promise.)

Frying tortillas, by contrast, are defined by a coarse grind and low moisture. Because they are eventually fried for tostadas (page 213) or totopos (page 215), for example, they are not exactly intended to be eaten after their initial bake. They are intentionally designed to absorb little oil, minimize blistering (which is the precursor to breakage, especially when packaged and shipped across long distances), and maximize crispiness. This makes for a brittle, dry finish that is under-whelming—if not mildly unpleasant—when eaten as is, but that will become sublime once fried.

Now, a note on blurred lines. Is this all to suggest that table tortillas aren't ever to be used for fried chips or that some frying tortillas, even unintentional ones, can't be fashioned into tacos?

Of *course* not. In fact, there are plenty of reasons to even support a hybrid approach between a table tortilla and a frying tortilla. At Masienda, for example, we ultimately decided to take the middle-ish ground when it came to formulating our own torti-lla—what the Lopez family uniquely refers to as a "recipe tortilla." A recipe tortilla is slightly coarser and dryer than a table tortilla and produces little to no puff. Because a tortilla puff creates a thin skin on one side of the tortilla as it expands with steam,

it can lead to tearing and breaking when reheated. For this reason, recipe tortillas are designed with food ser-vice in mind; they are fully capable of being reheated and folded into a taco and they also perform well in a fried or bathed (e.g., enchilada, enfrijolada, enmolada, etc.) application.

As far as table and frying tortillas go, this conversation doesn't even take into account the myriad regional and cultural preferences for masa around the globe. This is simply a way of map-ping the physical boundaries in which masa can possibly exist: fine/coarse, wet/dry. It's a simple continuum with lots of possibilities in between.

Table Tortilla (page 119)

Fine grind
High masa moisture (57–70%)
High finished-tortilla moisture (~47%)
Puffable

Frying Tortilla (page 135)

Coarse grind
Low masa moisture (45–55%)
Low finished-tortilla moisture (34%)
Not puffable

Perhaps because table tortillas are the most common masa application—always in seemingly ample, ready supply—the fresh masa used to make them is also used as a building block for several other dishes that we'll explore in this chapter, from memelas to tlayudas, and from sopes to certain kinds of tamales. (See page 88 for sifted wood ash preparation notes.) This main recipe shows you how to make masa from kernels, but you can skip directly to page 117 if you're starting with masa harina.

Table Tortilla Masa

MAKES 2.2 LB [998 G] MASA
(about thirty-five 5 in [15 cm] tortillas)

1 lb [455 g] dry field corn

⅛ oz [4.5 g] food-grade calcium hydroxide (1 percent cal to total weight of corn)

Warm water

INSTRUCTIONS

Rinse the corn in a colander to remove any debris or chaff.

Place the cal in a medium nonreactive mixing bowl and slowly incorporate warm water, stirring until the mix becomes a loose, smooth, and uniform slurry.

Pour the corn into a large nonreactive pot and add the cal mixture directly into the pot. Add just enough water to cover the corn by 4 in [10 cm] and stir everything together with a spatula to evenly incorporate.

Cover the pot (optional; however, it helps to get to temperature faster) and place over high heat. Bring to a boil, then lower the heat to medium for a simmer. Using a fine-mesh sieve, skim any unwanted kernels or particles that float to the surface and discard.

Stirring frequently so the corn doesn't scorch at the bottom of the pot, set a timer and check the corn every 5 minutes for the following variables:

→ Remove a kernel and rub it between your fingers. If the skin easily slides off (I mean *easily*), we're nearly there.

→ Taste a kernel. When it's ready, it will be tender, but al dente (like a boiled peanut or roasted cashew) and have a distinct tortilla flavor.

The skins' loosening and the texture and flavor development should take anywhere from 10 to 45 minutes, depending on the corn's moisture content and density.

Continue cooking, if necessary, checking every 5 minutes, until the skins are loosened and you have reached the desired texture and flavor. Remove from the heat and cover the pot. Let the pot sit undisturbed for 6 to 12 hours.

Drain the steeped corn, now called nixtamal, into a colander. Rinse, massage, and agitate the nixtamal vigorously until it has reached your desired percentage of skin wash-off (see page 90; I recommend about 50 percent, to start).

Grind the rinsed nixtamal (see page 92 for instructions). For a table tortilla masa, we want as fine a grind as possible—if you were to rub the masa between your fingers, the absolute ideal would be to feel no particles whatsoever.

Mix the masa manually or using a stand mixer with a dough hook attachment for 2 to 3 minutes, slowly adding water as needed, until the masa is as wet to the touch as possible without being sticky (that is, clumps should not easily stick to your hand). Perform the smush test (see page 116). Adjust the water as necessary until no cracking occurs.

cont'd

THE SMUSH TEST

To test the masa for the right level of moisture, roll a ping-pong-size ball (1½ in [4 cm]) and flatten it between the palms of your hands. If the edges of the flattened masa are cracking, add more water until it passes the same test without cracking. (The ideal texture is moist but not sticky, pliable but not gummy.) Once it does, you're ready to get into tortilla pressing.

Storage: Table tortilla masa contains 57 to 70 percent moisture, which means that it will ferment quickly at ambient temperatures. While I always prefer to use fresh masa immediately, you may choose to store it in the refrigerator for up to 3 days or in the freezer for up to 3 months. Bear in mind, however, that refrigerated or frozen masa will lose some elasticity over time, and you will most likely need to reincorporate additional moisture into the masa and mix it before use. If you are storing your masa at room temperature, I recommend holding for no longer than 4 hours. Even then, you may need to reincorporate a bit of moisture, as water will have evaporated from the masa, drying it out.

Preparing Table Tortilla Masa Using Masa Harina

If using masa harina (see Note, below), 1 lb [455 g] dry masa harina should yield 2 to 2½ lb [910 g to 1.2 kg] of wet masa.

By weight, you can assume the ratio of 1 part masa harina to 1.4 parts water. If you do not have a scale, 1 packed cup of masa harina requires about 1 scant cup [237 ml] of water (*by volume*). One packed cup of dry masa harina should yield about ten 5 in [15 cm] tortillas. Not all brands are created equal, so you may need to adjust ratios accordingly.

Slowly add the water to the dry masa harina in a large bowl, stirring the masa to incorporate evenly by hand (you may also choose to use a stand mixer fitted with a dough hook). Knead until the water is evenly incorporated and no dry, powdery spots remain. You'll want a finished masa that is moist to the touch, but not sticky.

Once prepared, use immediately, or rehydrate with additional water before use (if it's been more than a few minutes).

Note: This ratio was calculated using Masienda masa harina.

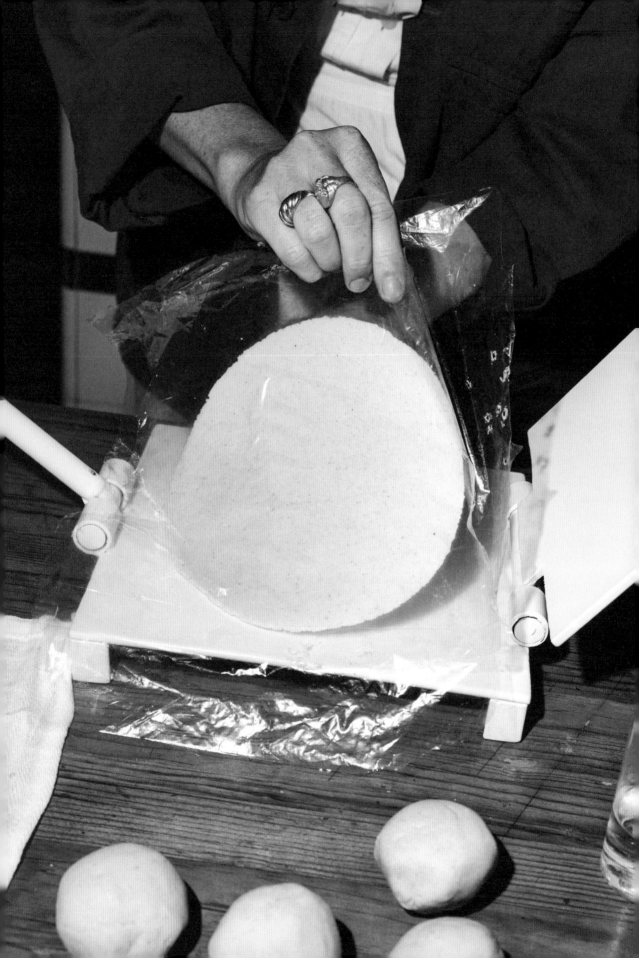

Now we're ready to portion and press our masa into table tortillas. There's something beautiful about this step that draws everyone—with or without cooking experience—to the prep table. It's fun and just technical enough to get you into an almost hypnotic focus. Table tortillas are also known as *tortillas blanditas* in Mexico, which translates to "soft tortillas."

Preparing the Table Tortilla

MAKES ABOUT THIRTY-FIVE 5 IN [15 CM] TORTILLAS

2.2 lb [998 g] Table Tortilla Masa (page 114)

Note: I like to pre-roll all of my masa into balls, so that the pressing and cooking processes that follow are streamlined. You may also save the pressed tortillas for later use. Some prefer to layer uncooked tortillas with wax paper in between and store in the refrigerator with a damp towel to cover. In our experience, rather than storing uncooked tortillas, we find it easier to par-cook the tortillas straight away and reheat later, adding a bit of water if necessary. Uncooked tortillas are not only more perishable, they are also more difficult to hydrate without mixing the masa all over again—and re-mixing would be a bummer if you've already taken the time to portion and shape each tortilla.

PRESSING THE TABLE TORTILLA
Preheat a comal to medium-low heat.

Open the tortilla press. Lay a plastic liner (see page 47) squarely on the surface of the press.

Break off about 2 Tbsp of fresh masa (or whichever size you prefer) and roll the masa into a ping-pong-size ball (1½ in [4 cm]) with your hands (see Note). Place the masa ball in the center of the plastic liner; to end up with a centered tortilla in the press, it sometimes helps to place the masa ball about 1 in [2.5 cm] from the center, closer to the press's hinge/pivot point. Place a second plastic liner on top of the masa ball.

With the top half of your fingers, slightly flatten the masa until it begins to adhere to the plastic liners (this prevents the masa from shifting around when you close the press).

Close the tortilla press lid and apply pressure by pushing down on the lever. Open the tortilla press lid and remove the flattened masa/uncooked tortilla. (You may first choose to flip the tortilla and press a bit more, if the tortilla is not as thin as you'd like. I like them to be about ¹⁄₁₆ in [1.5 mm].)

cont'd

For a decorative flourish, you can press flat herbs and flowers into the face of the tortilla at this stage. After the initial pressing, open the tortilla press lid, remove the top plastic liner, and place your herbs or flowers (for example, cilantro flower, hoja santa, tarragon) across the face of the tortilla (see photo above). Place the top plastic liner across the face of the tortilla (sealing in the herbs and/or flowers), close, and lightly press. Your garnish should now be nicely pressed into the tortilla.

For broad, large leaves, like hoja santa, for example, you may choose to apply a circle pastry cutter once the tortilla has been pressed and separated from the plastic liners to yield a more uniform finished shape.

Carefully peel away one plastic liner at a time. It helps to hold the tortilla face up (flat in your hand) and first carefully peel off the top liner; then, pinching one of the outer edges/corners of the plastic, flip the uncooked tortilla over to your opposing hand (the tortilla should now be directly touching your open-faced, opposing hand, ideally your pinky through middle fingers for best stability) and peel off the second plastic liner off.

COOKING THE TABLE TORTILLA

Raise the temperature of your preheated comal to medium heat. In a smooth, backhanded sweeping motion, place the uncooked tortilla directly on the nonstick surface. I prefer to put it directly onto the clean, dry surface; however, you can oil it if you prefer. Sear the first side for 20 to 30 seconds. I recommend using a timer, especially as you get a feel for your pan and the overall process. The hotter the temperature, the less time will be needed per side (even as little as 15 seconds, depending on how high the temperature is). The sear should yield a surface with even, light-colored spotting throughout. Flip and sear on the second side for another 20 to 30 seconds. Finally, flip the tortilla to its original seared side, allowing it to continue cooking through the center to your desired consistency and doneness. Play with sear times as you see fit.

I prefer table tortillas cooked to a medium internal moisture/doneness that passes the crumple test (see page 122)—that is, moist but not doughy and slightly molten on the inside, with a nice exterior crust. Even if you don't love a crust, keep in mind that this crust will soften quite a bit from steam if the tortilla is stacked in a pile and wrapped before serving. To reach this state, ideally the tortilla will have puffed during the cooking process (see The Table Tortilla Puff on page 126).

Note: If your tortilla did not start puffing after the initial sears on both sides, don't worry, you'll still have a mighty fine tortilla on your hands. Just be careful not to char the tortilla while you're waiting in vain for a puff—we aren't going for a tostada here!

Be sure to wipe your comal clean and dry after each use to prevent buildup (I almost always get a bit of masa somewhere on the surface somehow) or corroding.

If you intend to enjoy the tortilla immediately—as a snack, perhaps with a little salt and/or piece of avocado in the center—continue cooking for a bit longer. Once it's puffed for about 10 seconds, move the tortilla to the outside edge of your comal (if space allows) where it is slightly

cont'd

THE CRUMPLE TEST

One classic test for pliability is to crumple a tortilla in your fist, like a piece of paper, and then release it back onto a flat surface. You've reached table tortilla perfection if your tortilla unfurls with no cracking or breakage.

cooler, to let the tortilla continue cooking through the center for an additional 5 to 10 seconds per side. Transfer to a kitchen towel or tortilla warmer (tortillero) and allow the cooked stack of tortillas to steam for 5 minutes before serving. This will help prevent the tortillas from cracking.

If you plan to reheat the tortilla at some point later on—preferably within a couple of hours—it's best to remove the tortilla from the heat source once both sides have been seared and cooked through for a combined additional 15 seconds. By this point in the cooking process, it will be about 80 to 90 percent cooked. This will help ensure that you do not overcook the tortilla during the reheating process later on. Store in a kitchen towel or tortilla warmer if using within a few hours.

If you plan to refrigerate or freeze the tortillas for later use, cool the tortillas by fanning (that is, unstacking) them over a sheet pan (ideally with a cooling rack, to allow for ventilation). Once cooled to room temperature, place in a resealable plastic storage bag in the refrigerator for up to 7 days or in the freezer for up to 1 year.

To reheat tortillas: While I prefer reheating tortillas on a comal, there is no shame in reheating them in the microwave. Believe it or not, I've seen at least one ultra fine–dining restaurant group do just this. Some moisture loss will have occurred between the time the tortilla was first removed from the pan until now (whether stored ambient, refrigerated, or frozen), whether through steam or gradual evaporation. As the tortilla continues to cool, its gelatinized starch will begin to thicken and harden in texture. This process is known as retrogradation of starch. This can and will result in brittleness and/or cracking. We'll therefore want to incorporate a bit of moisture into the reheating process.

To reheat and/or revive a tortilla using a comal, first preheat the comal to medium-high heat. (Note: If beginning with a frozen tortilla, you may certainly put it directly onto the comal without wetting; however, I find it best to thaw it first and then proceed.) With an atomizer (on mist setting) or wet hands, lightly wet each side of the tortilla. Place the tortilla on the heated comal and heat for 20 to 30 seconds per side. Combined, the reintroduction of moisture and heat should render the tortilla pliable again. Transfer to a tortilla warmer and enjoy immediately.

To reheat in a microwave, wrap a tortilla inside of a kitchen towel (so that both sides of the tortilla are covered) and heat for 30 seconds.

Whether it be over a grill or in the microwave, you may choose to cook your tortilla on a range of cooking surfaces, not just a comal. Just keep in mind that the cook times will vary for each medium.

TORTILLAS PINTADAS ("PAINTED TORTILLAS"): Also known as *tortillas ceremoniales* ("ceremonial tortillas"), these stunning tortillas are customary among the Otomí people, for example, in the modern-day Mexican states of Querétaro and Guanajuato. Hand-carved wooden stamps with intricate patterns, shapes, and figures are used to apply edible paints to the face of the tortilla. The paints are most often derived from plants like hibiscus, marigold, beet, as well as cochineal, the insect from which preindustrial red dye was often derived. The stamp is applied once the tortilla is partially cooked, and the tortilla is finished on the comal to seal the dye. As the name implies, tortillas ceremoniales are offered on high religious and national holidays as well as special occasions such as weddings and quinceañeras.

The Table Tortilla Puff

Ah, the legendary tortilla puff. The puff is to tortilla making what the crumb is to bread baking.

Surely, you've seen that photo on the internet somewhere—the one where a baker proudly displays a loaf of bread that's been split down the center. With one hand taking the photo, their other hand is held out directly in front of them, mooning the camera with a cross section of their freshly baked boule. Spotted with holes like a block of Swiss cheese, the loaf's exposed interior, or crumb, reveals an intricate network of nooks and crannies that prove the baker's execution was on point (see page 224 for a nice-looking crumb).

While there's no doubt that a beautiful crumb is a cool thing to behold, its function is inextricably linked to its form. The fermentation used in sourdough creates little pockets of carbon dioxide, which expand throughout the unbaked loaf. The result, once baked and eaten, is an airy, dynamic texture that is light in bite and incredibly satisfying to chew. Add a nice crust on the outside, and you've got an enduring cultural phenomenon on your hands.

The same principle applies to a tortilla puff. Of course, we're not fermenting our masa, but we *are* preparing it in such a way that it ultimately expands when cooked, making for a pillowy, luxurious, ethereal bite.

Further, a puff ensures an even steam cooking through the center, which preserves internal moisture. This is necessary for pliability, a hallmark of a table tortilla.

You can imagine a tortilla that *doesn't* properly puff might take longer to cook through the center, likely leading to uneven, excessive cooking and dryness. Just think of searing a steak until it's well done—it is going to become tough and dry, with an overcooked exterior.

But note that the puff is truly necessary for only a handful of masa dishes prepared using a comal, most notably the panucho (page 185) and sometimes the gordita (page 171), depending on its style.

What's all this puff got to do with a table tortilla? A table tortilla is *often* one that puffs. It is the kind of tortilla that most of us are chasing, whether we know it or not, and now you'll have a detailed roadmap to get there.

PUFF LORE
According to a long-standing tradition throughout parts of Mesoamerica, women are deemed ready for marriage upon perfecting the single most sought-after and ethereal quality of the high masa arts: the tortilla puff.

ANATOMY OF A PUFF

A puff is made possible by trapped moisture that meets heat. The moisture is trapped by quickly searing a light crust onto both sides of the tortilla. Once the moisture and heat merge at the core, steam is created between the crusts, and pressure builds. That steam expands, causing the tortilla to puff like a balloon.

With this in mind, these are the five variables that will affect your puff:

(**Note**: If you are using store-bought masa harina, only items 3 through 5 will be relevant and/or within your control.)

1. **Grind**: A fine grind allows for even distribution and retention of moisture. Think of a whole corn kernel for a moment: if you were to add water to the kernel, it wouldn't absorb or retain very much moisture, if at all. This is obviously the most extreme example of a coarse grind, but it helps illustrate why even a masa grind with sea salt–sized kernel particles doesn't retain as much moisture as a smooth, fine grind (think Play-Doh) would. The finer the grind, the higher the moisture uptake, the more likely the puff.

2. **Elasticity**: As we covered earlier, the corn's outer skin, or pericarp, is where we find much of the kernel's natural gums. And while these gums can be a crucial element for binding the masa and ensuring that it does not fall apart, they are also important for producing a puff. When seared, a tortilla with some pericarp content creates an elastic skin/crust that helps trap and insulate moisture within its core. The more effectively moisture can be trapped within the center of the tortilla, the higher the steam pressure and the more robust your resulting puff.

3. **Moisture**: Moisture is so critical to coaxing a puff that large-scale tortillerias will often use lab-grade moisture meters to measure the masa's hydration level. This tool is expensive and not necessary to get the job done at home, but to give you an idea, a tortilleria's target moisture level for a puffable masa is typically 57 to 70 percent—that's a lot of moisture.

At home, I rely on look and feel. I take my masa to the upper limits of moisture, to the point *just before* I can't work it without it getting overly stuck to my fingers. And when cooking the tortilla, I want to see steam rising from the top of the tortilla.

You need ample moisture that can react with the heat to convert to steam and puff. If your masa has too little moisture, the tortilla in development will dry out before it can ever puff. A proper mixing/kneading process is critical to ensuring evenly distributed moisture. Additionally, I keep an atomizer or spray bottle handy for this very reason.

4. **Compression**: You don't technically need a thinly pressed tortilla for a puff. Look no further than a gordita (page 171), for example; this thick masa pancake will similarly puff like a table tortilla under the right conditions (its puff actually creates the pocket where you'd stuff it with delicious fillings, as you would with an arepa (page 155). But there is something to be said for the right amount of even compression—achieved during the pressing—on a table tortilla; this can help ensure a sufficient compaction of the moist masa, where steam pressure can later build and expand to form a puff. I like to press to a $1/16$ in [1.5 mm] thickness, which ensures a fairly quick, efficient cooking process. Keep in mind that the thicker the tortilla is, the more time it will need to cook.

5. **Temperature**: No heat, no puff. Remember, we are searing both sides of a table tortilla fast enough to trap moisture in the center, which will expand in the form of steam, as heat eventually reaches the tortilla's core. You want at least 400°F [200°C] (medium-high to high heat on your stovetop) to achieve this effect, though higher temperatures certainly won't hurt, when managed effectively. The wood-fired clay comales you'll find throughout Oaxaca, for example, average about 650°F [345°C]; tortilla conveyor ovens in tortillerias will cook at an average of about 500°F [260°C] between their various decks. This is all to say, table tortillas like it hot.

PUFF TROUBLESHOOTING

If you are having trouble getting your table tortilla to puff, here are some additional tips:

→ Following the second flip (when both sides have been seared and the tortilla's first seared side is face-down on the comal, see page 121), apply a bit of additional pressure to the surface of the tortilla with a flat spatula or your fingers to coax along the puffing process. You may also do this with your fingers wrapped in a kitchen towel. This can create just enough additional pressure to achieve liftoff.

→ When a tortilla won't puff, I find that moisture is most often the culprit, either before or during cooking. If your masa is too dry, it could be the result of 1) undercooked corn, 2) too coarse of a grind, or 3) not enough water added during grinding and/or mixing. In the simple case of insufficient water added during the mixing process, mix some more water into the masa and try again. Perform the smush test (see page 116) until the edges are no longer cracking. If your corn was indeed undercooked, there's no shortcut to fixing it. Better to recook a new batch and begin anew. As for the grind, give it another pass through your milling tool and see if you can't get it a bit smoother.

→ If you are working with prepared masa harina, moisture is also the most common culprit behind a lack of puff. Masa harina is generally quite finely ground, so grind won't likely be a factor. Just mix in a bit more water and do a quick smush test, repeating as necessary until it passes muster.

→ If you're searing either side for too long, you might be drying out the moisture in the center of the tortilla before that moisture has the chance to be trapped inside and work its magic. This is especially more likely with a higher heat and/or a thinner-pressed tortilla. Think of searing a thin burger patty or a fish to medium/medium-rare temp—these can be easy to overcook if you're not timing each side according to the surface temperature you're working with. Heat is, of course, necessary; just watch it closely.

→ When handling wet masa, it helps to also wet your hands. You'll almost never see a tortillerx in Mexico without a bucket of water nearby for rinsing and moistening their hands. This helps ensure that the masa doesn't stick to your hands over time; it also helps insulate it from the warmth and relative dryness of your masa-crusted hands, which will, believe it or not, gradually dry out the masa that you're handling.

→ I keep a spray bottle (i.e., atomizer) nearby to occasionally mist my tortillas with water while cooking, in order to ensure that they are never thirsty. If I'm working with a really hot comal (which causes the tortilla to dry out faster) or have noticed a bit of drying in the pressed masa (especially if the pressed masa was stored for any period in a refrigerator) before it is cooked, I'll sometimes spray the uncooked side of the tortilla that faces up as the other side begins its first sear.

→ If you're noticing that one side of your tortilla is inflating and the other is not, it's coming down to how you press the masa before it's cooked. It likely means that the tortilla is slightly thinner and more compressed on one side, so it cooks unevenly. I find it helps to flip the tortilla and press a second time, to ensure a more uniform thickness. Additionally, when pressing your tortillas, be careful not to rest your hand on one side of the press when holding the press for stability. I used to unconsciously do this in the beginning, and it would always lead to an uneven distribution of pressure and a partial puff.

→ Watch for little holes in the tortilla where the steam can escape. These will limit your puff potential. Holes and cracks are more likely to occur when your masa lacks sufficient moisture and/or has not been mixed thoroughly or evenly enough.

Frying Tortilla Masa

As a natural tortilla ages (sans preservatives), it loses moisture and gradually goes stale. This reduced moisture level allows it to fully crisp up in hot oil or the oven, so for eons, if we have ever wanted to make chips or tostadas at home, we would take slightly stale table tortillas from our counter or refrigerator and fry or bake them accordingly. This approach has stood the test of time because it works.

I nevertheless chose to include a note on preparing frying tortilla masa because, unbeknownst to most of us consumers, it is the foundation for a majority of the store-bought totopos and tostadas that are produced from nixtamal. In lieu of drying out premade table tortillas for several hours, tortillerias needed a faster way to achieve a dry tortilla that would fry as effectively, if not better. For some, the frying tortilla formulation was at least partially the result of the time and spatial limitations of storing day-old tortillas on the tortilla factory production floor. Although some places still produce their chips the old-fashioned way (albeit with a low-moisture, frying tortilla masa), they are comparatively more expensive to make and increasingly harder to find.

Frying tortillas simulate a stale tortilla by curbing moisture at three key points in the kernel-to-masa process. Beginning with cooking the corn, the kernels will likely be cooked a *touch* less than you might expect of a table tortilla. The corn is still cooked sufficiently to fully bloom its flavor, but the texture might be slightly grittier than *al dente* at the kernel's core.

As for the grind, a coarser grind is typical here, as is less water utilized during the grind itself (meaning a reduced trickle). Rather than a smooth, fine masa, you'll get one with little granulated bits of nixtamal, tip cap, and white starch, yielding a slight roughness when rubbed between your fingers. For this reason, frying tortilla masa is sometimes referred to as *masa quebrada* or "broken masa"—the masa is seen to be made of broken corn versus fully ground nixtamal.

The coarseness not only inhibits moisture uptake in the mixing process but also helps prevent excess oil absorption during the fry, leading to a less greasy chip or tostada. And, critically, a coarse grind discourages the bubbling and blistering that can occur during the fry, which minimizes chip and tostada breakage in storage, transport, or, most important, in guacamole- or salsa-dipping action.

Lastly, minimal water is added to frying tortilla masa during the mixing process. Mixing is still important, and some additional water may be necessary to ensure that the masa is workable, but little is needed compared to a table tortilla masa.

If the finished moisture percentage of a table tortilla is 47 percent, a frying tortilla's is closer to 30 percent. A frying tortilla is dry, a little gritty, and tough. Unlike a table tortilla, you won't exactly be craving a frying tortilla fresh off the comal. A little time in the fryer, though, and it earns its own place at the table.

MAKES 2.2 LB [998 G] MASA
(about thirty-five 5 in [15 cm] tortillas)

1 lb [455 g] dry field corn

⅙ oz [4.5 g] food-grade calcium hydroxide (or 1 percent cal to total weight of corn)

Warm water

INSTRUCTIONS

Rinse the corn in a colander to remove any debris or chaff.

Place the cal in a medium nonreactive mixing bowl and slowly incorporate warm water, stirring until the mix becomes a loose, smooth, and uniform slurry.

Pour the corn into a large nonreactive pot and add the cal mixture directly into the pot. Add just enough water to cover the corn by 4 in [10 cm] and stir everything together with a spatula to evenly incorporate.

Cover the pot (optional; however, it helps get to temperature faster) and place over high heat. Bring to a boil, then lower the heat to medium for a simmer. Using a fine-mesh sieve, skim any unwanted kernels or particles that float to the surface and discard.

Stir frequently so the corn doesn't scorch at the bottom of the pot. Set a timer and check the corn every 5 minutes for the following variables:

→ Remove a kernel and rub it between your fingers. If the skin easily slides off (I mean *easily*), we're nearly there.

→ Taste a kernel. When it's ready, it will be tender, but al dente (like a boiled peanut or roasted cashew) and have a distinct tortilla flavor. A tiny bit of grit is alright, as we're going for a slightly drier masa than that of a table tortilla.

The skins' loosening and the texture and flavor development should take anywhere from 10 to 45 minutes, depending on the corn's moisture content and density.

Continue cooking, if necessary, checking every 5 minutes, until the skins are loosened and you have reached the desired texture and flavor. Remove from the heat and cover the pot. Let the pot sit undisturbed for 6 to 12 hours.

cont'd

Drain the steeped corn, now called nixtamal, into a colander. Rinse, massage, and agitate the nixtamal vigorously until it has reached your desired percentage of skin wash-off (see page 90; I recommend about 50 percent, to start).

Grind the rinsed nixtamal (see page 92 for instructions). For a frying tortilla masa, we want a coarser grind, like coarse sea salt, so that if you rub the masa between your fingers, you feel particles of different textures, with enough moisture to hold the mixture together.

Mix the masa manually or using a stand mixer with a dough hook attachment for 2 to 3 minutes, slowly adding water as needed, until the masa is as wet to the touch as possible without being sticky (that is, clumps should not easily stick to your hand).

Perform the smush test (see page 116). Although we are going for a lower-moisture masa, we still want to ensure that it forms into an even, smooth shape when pressed. Adjust the water as necessary until no cracking occurs.

Storage: While I prefer to use fresh masa immediately, you may choose to store it in the refrigerator for up to 3 days or in the freezer for up to 3 months. Bear in mind, however, that refrigerated or frozen masa will lose some elasticity over time, and you will most likely need to incorporate additional moisture into the masa and mix it before use. If you are storing your masa at room temperature, I recommend holding for no longer than 4 hours. Even then, you may need to add a bit of moisture, as water will have evaporated from the masa, drying it out.

Preparing the Frying Tortilla

**MAKES ABOUT THIRTY-FIVE
5 IN [15 CM] TORTILLAS**

2.2 lb [998 g] Frying Tortilla Masa
(page 132)

PRESSING THE FRYING TORTILLA

Prepare the masa and press the tortillas following the
instructions on page 119.

While the same general method of pressing and cooking
a table tortilla applies to a frying tortilla, there are some
subtleties worth noting: For the press, consider how thick
you want your intended dish. Table tortillas are a bit more
forgiving because they are ultimately soft when served;
frying tortillas, by contrast, are served crispy for chips and
tostadas. Do you like a thin chip that's a bit more delicate,
or a thicker one that holds its own when smothered in a
chilaquiles or nachos application? Your desired thickness
will direct how much pressure you apply to the press. And
remember, once fried, the tortilla will change composition
and become firmer and, ideally, crispy. Too thick and you'll
have a hard time chewing; too thin and it will break at the
mere sight of guacamole.

COOKING THE FRYING TORTILLA

Raise the temperature of your preheated comal to
medium heat. In a smooth, backhanded sweeping motion,
place the uncooked tortilla directly on the nonstick surface (no oil needed). Sear the first side for 20 to 30 seconds. I recommend using a timer, especially as you get a
feel for your pan and the overall process. The hotter the
temperature, the less time will be needed per side (even
as little as 15 seconds, depending on how high the temperature is). The sear should yield a surface that looks like
the moon, with even, light-colored spotting throughout.
Flip and sear on the second side for another 20 to 30 seconds. Finally, flip the tortilla to its original seared side,
allowing it to continue cooking through the center to your
desired consistency and doneness. Play with sear times as
you see fit.

cont'd

I prefer frying tortillas cooked to a medium internal moisture/doneness that is moist but not doughy and slightly molten on the inside with a nice exterior crust. Although we want a low-moisture tortilla, we certainly don't want it to be stiff and inflexible. It probably won't pass the crumple test (see page 122) with flying colors, but a bit of pliability will help ensure that, once fried, the tortilla—even a thick one—isn't too brittle.

A brief rest (30 to 60 minutes) is advisable before frying. This allows any steam to dissipate, additional moisture to evaporate, and the tortilla to firm up a bit more before being dropped into the frying oil.

Unlike the table tortilla, we're not going for a puff here! Be careful not to char the tortilla by cooking too long, waiting in vain for a puff. You'll get a tostada this way, just not a very tasty one!

A 50/50 tortilla is an equal blend of both masa and wheat flour. I'll most often use this recipe in a breakfast taco application. I'm also partial to coconut oil for its sweetness, but you can use butter, lard, or another fat substitute, if you prefer.

50/50 Tortillas

MAKES ABOUT EIGHT 10 IN [30 CM] OR SIXTEEN 5 IN [15 CM] TORTILLAS

1 cup [150 g] Masa Harina

1 cup [140 g] all-purpose flour

1 tsp salt

1 tsp baking powder

⅓ cup [75 g] solid coconut oil (or preferred fat substitute)

1 cup [240 ml] warm water

Combine the dry ingredients in a large bowl and add the coconut oil. Mix until well combined and small crumbles begin to form. Add the warm water and mix well. The dough should be oily and not stick to your hands.

Knead for 2 to 4 minutes on a lightly floured surface. Shape the dough into 8 (large) or 16 (small) balls, cover, and let rest for 30 minutes.

Preheat the comal to medium-high heat. Press a dough ball using a tortilla press (see page 119).

Lower the comal to medium heat and, in a smooth, backhanded sweeping motion, place the uncooked tortilla directly on the nonstick surface (no oil needed).

Let it cook for approximately 20 to 25 seconds until it begins to release itself from the comal. Flip and cook the other side for about 20 seconds. Flip again, and you should begin to see the tortilla puff.

A bit of char is to be expected and especially adds to this tortilla's charm. Allow the tortilla to continue cooking through to the center (about 20 seconds). When done, transfer to a kitchen towel or tortilla warmer and allow the cooked stack of tortillas to steam for 5 minutes before serving. This will help prevent the tortillas from cracking. Repeat with the remaining dough balls.

If you plan to reheat and enjoy the tortillas later, see instructions on pages 122–23.

Masa for Tamales

Tamales are wrapped masa cakes, often stuffed with meats, vegetables, and herbs, and wrapped with ingredients ranging from banana leaves, to corn husks (fresh and dried), leafy greens, reed, and even plastic wrap. The word *tamal* is derived from the Nahuatl word *tamalli*, which means "unformed corn dough."

Much like masa for tortillas, masa for tamales is largely differentiated by texture. To this end, two more widely known masa genres tend to dominate the tamal canon (though they are certainly not the only two):

MASA CERNIDA

At one tamal extreme, you have, for example, the spongey, cake-like tamales found throughout central and northern Mexico, made of ground (often coarsely so) dried nixtamal. Though most popularly associated with pozole, the ultra-floury cacahuazintle varietal is often the corn of choice for this kind of masa, especially in the immediate region around Mexico City. In Mexico, this kind of masa is often referred to as *masa cernida* ("sifted masa"). It is derived from well-rinsed, nixtamalized corn that is then partially dehydrated, ground with either a traditional molino or stone rollers, and oftentimes sifted, as the name suggests. If you've ever been to a tortilleria that has a big bin of dry-looking masa for scooping by the pound or kilo, that's the stuff.

For Masa Cernida, follow instructions for Masa Harina (page 147), using the cacahuazintle landrace as your corn varietal of choice.

MASA REFREGEDA

At the other end of the spectrum, you'll encounter tamales that seem to be more about the filling than the masa itself. So much so that the masa might constitute little more than a thin layer between the filling and the wrapper, which might be just a smooth banana leaf. The masa—also made of nixtamal, but more commonly with corn varieties that are denser than a pozolero (that is, a varietal of corn used commonly for pozole)—is a very fine grind like that you'd expect of a table tortilla masa. In fact, the same masa for table tortillas will be typically used for this kind of tamal. This masa style is more prevalent throughout southern Mexico (in places like Oaxaca, Chiapas, Veracruz, and Yucatán) and parts of Central America. It can have an almost fudge-like texture; it's dense and slightly gelatinous at times. Those tamales that consist of nixtamal that has been fully washed (that is, 100 percent skin wash-off)—referred to as *masa refregada* ("scrubbed masa")—will yield a finished tamal that is decidedly smoother and less gelatinous than one prepared with a lower wash-off percentage.

For Masa Refregada, follow instructions for Table Tortilla Masa (page 114).

Note: When rinsing the nixtamal, be sure to wash the skins off entirely, as this masa's name suggests.

Regardless of the texture of the masa, these two types of tamales almost always involve some combination of masa, fat (usually asiento, or lard), seasoning, and often, though not always, filling. When in doubt as to what ratio to assume, give 2-2-1-1 a try. As our friends at Guelaguetza restaurant in Los Angeles showed us, 2-2-1-1 stands for: 2 cups masa harina to 2 cups of broth (or water) to 1 cup of fat to 1 teaspoon of baking powder, with salt to taste. If using table tortilla masa, you can skip the fat, baking powder, and salt, while incorporating just enough additional broth or water to achieve a sticky but easily spreadable masa (about 10 to 20 percent more moist than a Table Tortilla Masa).

Again, these are not the only two kinds of masa for tamales. For example, some variations involve slightly fermented masa. Others—like the humitas of South America, which use fresh corn; the tamales of Cuba and parts of the Caribbean, which use corn flour, and even certain kinds of tamales in Mexico that use plain-cooked corn—don't call for traditional masa at all.

Most wrapped tamales are fairly labor intensive, and many are considered a special-occasion food, so it is recommended that you make several at a time in order to justify the prep.

According to one estimate, there are around three hundred kinds of tamales in Mexico alone. While we won't be covering any specific tamal recipe per se, these masa approaches should provide the base for you to tackle any that you see fit.

COLADOS
The colados of the Yucatán are partially derived from masa but eschew the dough itself almost entirely. In this process, a blend of approximately equal parts water and masa are mixed together and strained of the liquid. That liquid is then set to reduce gradually over a low heat, creating a thick, starchy purée that sets into a gelatin of sorts once cooled. This gelatin is placed atop various ingredients, oftentimes chicken, then wrapped and steamed before being served.

Pozole (a.k.a. Masa in Development)

Though pozole is not exactly masa, I decided to include a quick recipe because it is essentially washed nixtamal only one short step away from becoming masa. This means that if you are preparing masa for tortillas, you can also experiment with making pozole by saving some whole (unground), rinsed (I like 100 percent wash-off of the skins) nixtamal and cooking it further until it fully tenderizes and expands.

Pozole can be found in one form or another all across the Americas. It is also referred to as mote (in much of South America), hominy (United States), rockahomonie and sagamite (Algonquin), sofki (Creek), and tanlubo and tafala (Choctaw).

Pozole is a celebration food in Mexico, most often enjoyed during the fall and winter holidays such as Mexican Independence Day, Christmas, and New Year's Eve. Pozole refers to both the nixtamalized corn within the dish as well as the completed dish itself. In the olden days, its preparation was closely tied to ritual human sacrifices in Mesoamerican culture. Whereas today, braised pork is the most commonly included protein, let's just say that, back then, the name of the protein sounded a lot like *cumin*.

In addition to serving as a starchy base for soups, pozole can be treated much like a pasta—such as the *pozole seco* of Colima—or fried, like *pozole frito*, which is tossed stir-fry style in a pan with a protein of some kind.

Note: One notable pozole stronghold is in Jalisco, Mexico, where elotes occidentales and maíz ancho are grown. Cacahuazintle, however, is perhaps the most common varietal of pozole corn. With its soft, floury starch and large kernel size, cacahuazintle blooms into a beautiful addition to any soup or stew, especially when its tip cap (attachment point to the cob) is severed during the unique shelling process using a circular saw.

PREPARE THE NIXTAMAL

Option #1 (longer method): I prefer this method, if I have the time, because the additional nixtamalization time really develops the flavor of the corn. And, if I'm already making nixtamal for masa, why not? Varietals like bolita, olotillo, and tuxpeño are some of my favorites for tackling both a masa and pozole application with the same batch. Follow the instructions for preparing Table Tortilla Masa (page 114) until you have your nixtamal. Set aside as much as you'd like (about ½ cup to 1 cup [90 g to 180 g] per serving, depending on your appetite) and rinse vigorously until no skins remain (i.e., 100 percent wash-off). Continue to Prepare the Pozole (page 146).

Option #2 (shorter method): Follow the instructions for preparing Table Tortilla Masa (page 114) until your corn is ready to be removed from the heat (the skins easily come off and the flavor has begun to bloom). Do *not* let the nixtamal continue to steep for 6 to 12 hours; instead, immediately strain the nixtamal through a colander and begin rinsing vigorously until no skins remain (i.e., 100 percent wash-off). Continue to Prepare the Pozole.

cont'd

Note: Before preparing the pozole, you may choose to remove the tip cap individually from each kernel. While not necessary, this is sometimes done in order to encourage the kernel to bloom in greater size during its second cook.

PREPARE THE POZOLE

Fill a separate pot with enough water to cover the nixtamal with about 2 in [5 cm] of water. Bring to a boil over high heat, then lower to a simmer (medium-high heat). Add the rinsed nixtamal and cook until it softens to your desired texture (between 2 and 6 hours). Serve with any soup or pozole broth recipe you enjoy most. I often use a simple chicken broth, sometimes plain, other times with the corn broth and some ground chiles thrown in for heft and heat.

Storage: For either preparation option, once the skins have been washed off, you may choose to freeze the pozole (which, at this point, is parcooked) for up to one year. Refrigerated pozole is best eaten within one week of preparation.

Masa Harina

Masa harina ("masa flour") is dehydrated masa. If fresh masa is produced at about a 57 percent moisture level, masa harina, by contrast, has around an 11 percent moisture level. This low moisture level gives masa harina shelf stability for weeks, months, and even years, whereas fresh masa is perishable within a matter of days or even hours, depending on how it is stored.

While most commercial masa harina producers employ a process more or less similar to the traditional method of making masa (slow food), there are slight modifications to the system that allow manufacturers to manipulate the masa's presentation and/or accelerate the process, thereby saving money and maximizing margins (fast food).

To manipulate color, white corns are typically degermed before nixtamalization, which also reduces the natural nutrient density of the corn. Further, some large-scale manufacturers of masa harina often bleach the corn with citric acid or phosphoric acid to achieve the most pure white masa possible (white masa harina making up about 60 percent of the market). Finally, the masa is flash dried in a furnace at temperatures upward of 750°F [400°C] for about 4 seconds, which can lead to a denaturing of the masa's nutrients. Some research on grain-based pasta, for example, suggests that such high temperatures diminish the nutritional value of otherwise nutrient-dense grains.

Most masa harina is manufactured for food service use, primarily tortillerias and snack producers. According to one industry insider, the best masa harina goes to these customers, while the "seconds" (that is, the heads and tails of production, usually of lower quality) are packaged and distributed to the retail market.

Since its introduction to the United States and Mexico in the early and mid-twentieth century, respectively, masa harina has competed directly with the traditional method of masa production, leading to an enormous shift in the way masa is accessed across the world. Of course, there are both pros and cons to this convenience.

While masa harina is most efficiently produced at mass scale, it can also be created in the home kitchen, in case you are so inclined.

PREPARATION

Method #1: Follow the instructions for preparing Table Tortilla Masa (page 114) until you have your nixtamal. Preheat the oven to 275°F [135°C]. Take fresh nixtamal that has been washed as you prefer. Spread evenly across a full oven rimmed baking sheet. Bake until the nixtamal is dried through the center of the kernels, about 4 hours. Remove and let cool to room temperature. Grind with a tabletop grain mill or hand-cranked mill. For the hand mill, you may need at least two passes before it is sufficiently ground.

cont'd

Method #2: Preheat the oven to 275°F [135°C]. Take fresh masa (see Table Tortilla Masa, page 114) and spread evenly across a full oven rimmed baking sheet. Bake for 2 hours. Remove the pan and carefully flip the now-developed cake. Return the pan to the oven and bake for another 2 hours, or until fully baked and dry through the center. Let cool. Break into chunks and, in small batches, place into a blender (preferably a Vitamix). Pulse in the blender until it is a fine powder.

Storage: Masa flour prepared with either method (homemade, not store-bought masa harina) can be stored for up to one month in an airtight container. It may last longer, depending on the moisture content (store-bought masa is around 11%), and you may choose to also include a desiccant packet in the container for extended freshness.

I once read that there are about three hundred and fifty different shapes for pasta, with four times as many names.

While I have yet to find a similar survey for masa specifically, there are reports of more than *six hundred* documented, traditional dishes that use corn in Mexico alone. And, given the significance of traditional-method masa in Mexican culture, it stands to reason that most of these dishes are derived from nixtamalized corn dough in some way.

Of course, this doesn't even take into account the extent of variations in either the dish names, their finished compositions, or their countries of origin. For example, the soft taco, as we know it, might indeed count as one of these six hundred dishes, but exactly how many taco possibilities are there in Mexico? How about in the United States? Japan? Seeing as how you can make a taco out of just about anything, anywhere, you're looking at limitless variations on the theme.

As dynamic as the masa canon is, however, it is not necessarily amorphous. There is a relatively finite number of traditional shapes that we can draw upon for inspiration, with infinite possibilities, traditional and otherwise, to be made from them.

What follows here is a dossier of sorts on the more iconic masa shapes occurring throughout Mexico, Central America, South America, and even the United States (home of the puffy taco), each with instructions on basic preparation. I won't go into detail on their traditional toppings or fillings, since these vary greatly, but I will include a general guide of ideas on how to

get you there. I encourage you to explore traditional and nontraditional approaches to each of these shapes, perhaps even adding your own figures to the mix, if you're feeling extra creative.

A few cooking style notes:

→ Unless otherwise indicated, each of these shapes assumes a Table Tortilla Masa base (page 114). A finer, moister masa is both easier to shape and much more delicious in a comal application (i.e., dry-heat comal as opposed to fried or boiled). If you want to experiment with Frying Tortilla Masa (page 132), your best bet is to do so with some of the fried applications, particularly the hard-shell taco (page 173), totopo (page 215), and tostada (page 213).

→ You are welcome to use masa harina (see page 117) for any of these shapes. In fact, I'd encourage you to start with masa harina for ease and practice! Once you have the techniques down, you can transition into making your own masa for these applications. A note on masa harina: Because of how finely ground masa harina is, it will invariably absorb more oil in fried applications, becoming quite light, bubbly/blistered, and delicate as a result. If you are used to a heartier bite, you'll want to use either Frying Tortilla Masa (page 132) or freshly-ground Table Tortilla Masa (page 114).

→ If using a comal, you can experiment with adding a bit of oil (or any other fat) or not. Because a seasoned comal is naturally nonstick, I do not usually call for oil, but a little extra fat is never a bad thing in my book.

→ The colors of corn/masa that you use are entirely up to you.

→ It helps to have a bowl of water nearby when making these shapes, so you can easily dip your hands to prevent masa sticking or drying out while being shaped.

→ I suggest sizes for each dish (for example, "roll a ping-pong-size masa ball"), but you can scale these up or down as you see fit.

→ Masa dishes are best enjoyed fresh, but leftovers deserve love too.

Recipe Key

ROOTS: This indicates the location with which the shape is most popularly associated, though regional overlap is bound to occur and all associated regions are not necessarily highlighted.

FORMAT: With the exception of atole (a beverage), this is mostly a binary system—each shape is either a stuffer, stuffed with something, or a topper, topped with something (a few shapes can serve as either). Very technical terms, indeed.

COOKING METHOD: Depending on the application, each shape can be cooked in at least one of the following ways: comal (pan, griddle, plancha), fried (deep, shallow, air), boiled, simmered, grilled, or baked. **Note:** For recipes that call for frying, I use a neutral vegetable oil.

INTRO: Some regional variations are acknowledged here, whether in name or presentation, as well as additional context and fun facts.

INSTRUCTIONS: This is the suggested way to bring this shape to life. What you do with it from there is entirely up to you!

STORAGE: Some masa shapes lend themselves better to storage than others. I'll make a note on each shape's shelf life here.

For additional information on how to prepare each shape, visit Masienda's YouTube channel at youtube. com/masienda.

Arepa

A thick, stuffed masa pocket that *kind of* resembles an uncut English muffin and *really* resembles a gordita (page 171)

ROOTS: Venezuela, Colombia

FORMAT: Stuffer

COOKING METHOD: Comal

Today, arepas are most commonly made with a specific kind of corn flour that is sold as harina precocida or masa arepa. Arepas of this kind are known as arepas piladas (with an *i*). To produce masa for arepas piladas, dry corn (a soft, floury type commonly called cariaco) is pounded until the skins begin to separate from the kernels. The skins are then mechanically removed and discarded before the broken kernels are cooked in water, strained, ground into a dough, and, finally, dehydrated. Some popular masa arepa brands you'll encounter are Harina P.A.N., Areparina, and Masarepa.

Nevertheless, a nixtamal-based masa substitution is applicable here and is, in fact, used in arguably the most traditional form of arepas: arepas peladas (with an *e*). Traditional-method masa in arepas goes back to ancient times. While not as common, arepas peladas and raspadas—both arepas made from nixtamal, often prepared with wood ash—are still very much a thing in Venezuela and Colombia. Grind coarseness may vary, but a table tortilla masa will work well in this application.

INSTRUCTIONS

Roll a ball of Table Tortilla Masa (page 114) the size of a racquetball (about 2 in [5 cm]). Flatten into a ½ in [12 mm] thick disk with your hands.

Preheat a nonstick pan over medium-high heat. Cook one side of the arepa for about

3 minutes. A nice, lightly colored crust should start to form on the cooked side. Flip the arepa to the uncooked side and cook for another 3 minutes. Continue cooking for another minute or so on each side until cooked through the center. To avoid overcooking the arepa's exterior, you can also finish the last bit of cooking (2 to 4 minutes) in the oven preheated to 400°F [200°C]. A soft, cooked, molten center is the goal.

Remove from the heat. While still warm, use the tip of a paring knife to cut a horizontal slit through the top layer of the arepa. Holding the sides of the arepa with one hand, gently work the middle three fingers of your opposite hand through the slit and wiggle your fingers to open the pocket.

Fill the inside with any stuffing you'd like—stewed meats, cheeses, or vegetables. I've enjoyed arepas throughout Venezuela, but my favorite arepa of all time comes from a restaurant called Caracas Arepa Bar in New York. Known as "La del Gato," it's stuffed with fried sweet plantains, avocado slices, and Guayanés cheese and topped with a sweet-hot "secret sauce."

Storage: Arepas (without filling) should keep for up to 7 days refrigerated or 1 year frozen. A little bit of water rubbed on either side of the arepa will help replenish any moisture lost during storage, prior to reheating on a comal.

Atole

A masa-based beverage that resembles a porridge or gruel

ROOTS: Mexico

FORMAT: Sipper

COOKING METHOD: Simmered

The word *atole* is derived from the Nahuatl word *atolli*. Plain atole is a staple of Yucatán, Tabasco, and Oaxaca and is the result of liquefying masa, traditionally with water, though milk may also be used. Given the true simplicity of this dish, it's not hard to imagine it being among the earliest Mesoamerican culinary staples; it is nutritious, highly caloric, and easy to flavor in myriad ways. In its simplest form, atole is masa and water, combined and brought to a simmer. That said, not all atoles are necessarily masa based; rice and wheat, for example, are sometimes substituted.

Atole's texture and flavor vary according to region, season, personal preference, and supply (thin atoles are common when corn inventory is scarce). Chile atole, for example, is a savory atole preparation with chiles and salt; champurrado, derived from the word *champurrar* ("to mix"), is a sweet atole infused with cacao, sugar, and sometimes additional spices like cinnamon. Champurrado is similar to the Yucatecan variation of atole tanchucuá, which may incorporate maíz nuevo (a slightly sweeter "new corn" that has not fully dried and matured) and additional ingredients like black pepper, anise, and allspice. From Tabasco, pozol (or chorote, when mixed with cacao) is a variation on atole that uses fermented masa as its base. And of course, there's tejuino, a refreshing fermented masa drink served chilled with lime, salt, and chile, common throughout Jalisco and northern Mexico. While technically not always made of masa, the tascalate of Chiapas is made of corn, cacao, achiote, cinnamon, and oftentimes toasted and ground tortillas.

INSTRUCTIONS

In a large pot over high heat, add 1 part Table Tortilla Masa (page 114) to 3 parts boiling water (5 parts, if using dry masa harina). Lower the heat to medium. Whisk continuously until the masa is evenly incorporated and smooth. Incorporate any spices or flavors. If you desire a thicker atole, continue cooking, stirring frequently, until sufficiently reduced; if you desire a thinner consistency, gradually add water, stirring frequently, until the desired consistency is reached. Atole is best served warm.

Storage: While atole is best enjoyed immediately, you can refrigerate in an airtight container for up to 24 hours. After 24 hours, it will become gritty, even after rehydrating and reheating. Upon reheating, it is best to rehydrate the atole as needed. There is no specific amount of liquid recommended for reheating; just thin the atole out a bit, stirring constantly, and cook until it reduces to your desired consistency.

Bollo

A stuffed masa ball-shaped dumpling

ROOTS: Venezuela

FORMAT: Stuffer and topper

COOKING METHOD: Boiled, simmered

Bollo is the Spanish word for "bun." These are like stuffed, boiled molotes (page 183) or steamed masa dumplings and are especially tasty topped with a fresh tomato sauce and grated Cotija or Parmesan cheese. Though bollos are not necessarily always stuffed, I find that the best versions do contain a filling. The most common filling is a ground beef picadillo, but, as with dumplings of all cultures, anything goes, really. Just be sure to cook the filling ahead of time, as our goal is to heat the filled bollo through to the center (but not necessarily complete cooking of the filling from a raw state).

This being a Venezuelan dish, it is more common to use P.A.N. or some other brand of arepa flour with boiled (not nixtamalized) corn as its base, but traditional masa will get the job done brilliantly. As it does for chochoyotes (page 165), the masa for bollos often includes a bit of fat and salt, but this part is totally up to you. If using fat, like vegetable oil, I recommend beginning with 10 percent as much fat weight as total masa weight (1:10 ratio). If you plan to shape and then immediately freeze them, a bit of fat mixed into the masa will help preserve the integrity of the bollos through the eventual thaw. I enjoy them both with and without the additional fat; I season them with the cooking water, which I salt as I would any pasta water (that is, like the ocean).

INSTRUCTIONS

Roll a ping-pong-size (1½ in [4 cm]) ball of Table Tortilla Masa (page 114). Press your fingertip into the center, creating an indentation about a third to halfway into the ball. Gently pack your filling into the crater, taking care to not overfill past the ridge of the opening. With moist hands, gradually sculpt the edges upward until they meet over the top, enclosing the stuffing at the center of what should still look like a ball. Place on a baking sheet and cover with a damp kitchen towel.

Bring a pot of water to a boil and season with salt. Line a plate or tray with paper towels. Carefully drop the bollos from the baking sheet into the pot. Cook for about 10 minutes, or until warm through the center. Using a slotted spoon or spider, transfer to a folded paper towel to drain. Top with tomato sauce, salsa, soy sauce, or any other condiments that appeal and serve immediately. These are best served warm.

Storage: If freezing the bollos, it is best to do so before boiling them. You can freeze uncooked bollos for up to a year or refrigerate for up to 3 days. Cooked bollos can be refrigerated for up to 7 days in an airtight container or resealable plastic bag.

Cazuelita

A dimpled fried dumpling made with masa, potatoes, and sometimes cheese

ROOTS: Mexico (Nuevo León)

FORMAT: Topper

COOKING METHOD: Fried

Cazuelita is the Spanish diminutive word for "pot." As the name and appearance suggest, these cazuelitas take their shape from traditional clay pots you'll commonly find in Mexico. They look like chochoyotes (page 165), only slightly larger and fried. Cheese in the masa is definitely not a dealbreaker with this dish, but I personally prefer the masa mix to be prepared without it. A common cazuelita topping is a picadillo of ground beef.

INSTRUCTIONS

Mix equal parts (by weight) wet masa and boiled, mashed potatoes (I like them peeled, but this step is optional) and salt to taste.

Roll a slightly smaller than ping-pong-size (1 in [2.5 cm]) ball of Table Tortilla Masa (page 114). Press your fingertip into the center, creating an indentation about a third to halfway into the ball. Place on a baking sheet and cover with a damp kitchen towel.

Heat 2 to 3 in [5 to 7.5 cm] of oil to 350°F [180°C] and fry the cazuelitas until golden brown, 3 to 4 minutes. (They can also be pan-fried in enough oil to cover the bottom of the pan.) A little white spot in the cazuelita's indentation is normal, even when fully cooked. The ideal finished texture is crispy on the outside and molten on the inside. Transfer to a folded paper towel to drain, indentation facedown.

Fill the indentation of the cazuelita with any fillings you desire and serve while warm.

Storage: Cazuelitas are best enjoyed immediately and do not store well once cooked. If preparing ahead of time, you can freeze the cazuelitas, uncooked, for up to 1 year. You can also refrigerate them (uncooked) for up to 3 days; however, they will dry out slightly over time.

Chalupa

An oblong, ridged masa vessel

ROOTS: Mexico (Estado de México, Puebla, Guerrero)

FORMAT: Topper

COOKING METHOD: Comal, fried

In Mexico, the translation of *chalupa* is "small canoe." Thus, one version of the chalupa (pictured) is a more literal canoe-shaped piece of masa, meant for filling: a log with a long depression along the top. Another flatter version seems less strictly inspired by the canoe shape, often resembling a cross between a sope (page 199) and a huarache (page 177) or a tlacoyo (page 205).

So, the chalupa shape is quite varied and a bit tricky to pin down. One version from Puebla, chalupas poblanas, are essentially fried tostadas smothered with salsas and meats. In nearby Guerrero, chalupitas or "little chalupas" are little hand-shaped bowls of fried masa. And then there's the infamous Taco Bell chalupa, which more closely resembles the puffy taco shells of San Antonio, Texas (page 187).

INSTRUCTIONS
Preheat the comal to medium-high heat. Roll a 1 to 2 in [2.5 to 5 cm] ball of Table Tortilla Masa (page 114) and then roll it into a log shape, 4 to 6 in [10 to 15 cm] long. Using the tip of your finger, create an indentation across the top length of the log. This ensures that your chalupa retains sauces and additional toppings later on.

Lower the comal heat to medium. Cook the ridged side of the chalupa for about 2 minutes. Flip over and let the second side cook for another 2 to 3 minutes. Flip the chalupa back to the ridged side for another 2 minutes. Continue cooking until cooked through to the center but still soft, about 6 minutes total.

For the best fried chalupa results, I recommend that you par-cook the chalupa on a comal for 2 minutes per side, then fry to golden brown in oil at 350°F [180°C]. These are best served warm.

For the chalupa poblana, refer to the Tostada recipe (Fried subsection) on page 213.

Storage: Enjoy immediately, or, if planning to use within the next 6 to 12 hours, let rest wrapped in a kitchen towel at room temperature. Cooked chalupas (without toppings) should store for up to 7 days in the refrigerator or 1 year frozen. Prior to reheating with a comal, a little bit of water rubbed on either side of the chalupa will help replenish any moisture lost during storage.

Chochoyote

A masa dumpling the shape of a large "innie" belly button

ROOTS: Mexico (Oaxaca, Veracruz)

FORMAT: Topper

COOKING METHOD: Boiled, simmered, fried

These are also known as *ombligitos* ("little belly buttons") in Veracruz. Often boiled and even sometimes fried, they are usually added to soups, stews, and pots of beans. Traditional chochoyotes fold a bit of fat and salt into the masa, but this is totally up to you. If using fat, like vegetable oil, I recommend beginning with 10 percent fat weight of total masa weight (1:10 ratio). If you plan to shape and then immediately freeze them, a bit of fat mixed into the masa will help preserve the integrity of the chochoyotes through the eventual thaw. I enjoy them both with and without the additional fat, and season them instead within the cooking water, which I salt as I would a pasta water (as salty as the ocean).

INSTRUCTIONS

Roll a slightly smaller than ping-pong-size (1 in [2.5 cm]) ball of Table Tortilla Masa (page 114). Press your fingertip into the center, creating an indentation about a third to halfway into the ball. Place on a baking sheet and cover with a damp kitchen towel.

Bring a pot of water to a boil and season with salt. Carefully drop the chochoyotes from the baking sheet into the pot. Boil for about 10 minutes, or until cooked through the center. Drain in a colander and use immediately in soups, stews, or beans, or finish as you would a gnocchi or pasta dish. Chochoyotes are best served warm.

Storage: Uncooked, the chochoyotes can be frozen for up to 1 year or refrigerated for up to 3 days.

Empanada

A fried masa turnover, often stuffed with meat filling

ROOTS: Spain (wheat flour), Mexico (masa)

FORMAT: Stuffer and topper

COOKING METHOD: Deep-fried, comal

The original Spanish empanada uses wheat flour, not masa—but this being a book on masa, the corn dough of Meso-american origin, I offer a recipe for the Mexican version instead. The name is derived from the Spanish word *empanar* ("to bread"). Spanish colonialism made empanadas ubiquitous throughout Latin America, where they may be made of wheat, corn, or plantain dough, and baked or fried.

While you can certainly bake a masa empanada, I find that the texture is not quite as crisp and satisfying as you get with a fried one. At least one notable exception is the empanada de mole amarillo (a yellow mole empanada) in Oaxaca, which is prepared on the comal, much like a quesadilla.

INSTRUCTIONS

Roll a ping-pong-size ball (about 1½ in [4 cm]) of Table Tortilla Masa (page 114) or Frying Tortilla Masa (page 132) and load into a tortilla press. Following the same process as for a Table Tortilla (page 119) or Frying Tortilla (page 135), apply slight pressure to your press to make a tortilla about ⅛ in [3 mm] thick. Remove the top sheet of plastic wrap and load the filling into the center of the tortilla, leaving room around the edges for a clean seal. Pack with enough filling to ensure an even, hearty stuffing, but take care to not overdo it—you want to be able to neatly fold the empanada without rupturing. Lightly wet the outer edges of the tortilla to seal.

Lift any edge of the bottom plastic sheet to fold the tortilla over itself into a half moon–shaped turnover. Use your fingers or the tines of a fork to gently press and seal the edges, ensuring that the filling is securely packed inside.

Heat 4 in [10 cm] of oil to 350°F [180°C] and fry the empanadas until golden brown and crispy. (They can also be pan-fried in enough oil to cover the bottom of the pan.) These are best served warm.

Storage: A fried empanada is best enjoyed immediately, while hot; they do not store well. Uncooked, they can be frozen for up to 1 year or refrigerated for up to 3 days.

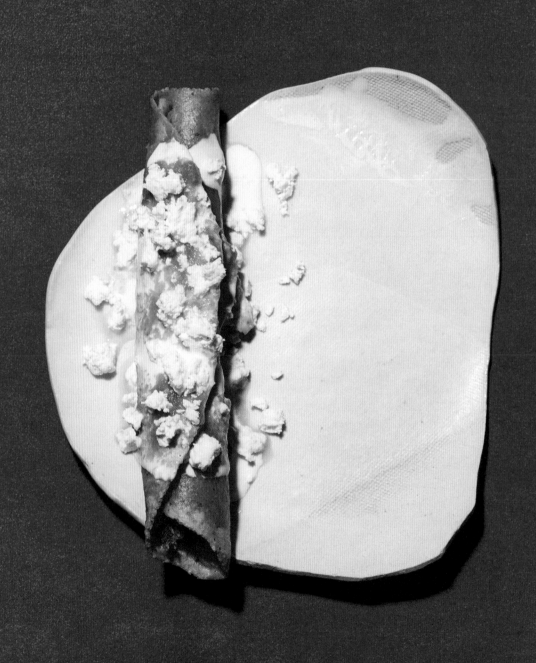

Flauta
(Tacos Dorados, Taquitos)

A rolled, fried taco, much resembling a flute . . . or a stick of dynamite
(see Soft-Shell Taco, page 197)

ROOTS: Mexico

FORMAT: Always a stuffer, sometimes also a topper

COOKING METHOD: Deep-fried

Crisp and delicious, flautas (Spanish for "flute") are a perfect appetizer, snack, or full meal. Some kind of meat filling, like shredded chicken or carne asada, is most common, and they are often topped with some combination of crema, guacamole salsa, chile salsa, iceberg lettuce, runny refried beans, and queso fresco.

Although I recommend pressing a tortilla shape first, thin huarache-shaped tortillas (see page 177) are also used for flautas, which give a bit more surface area for stuffing and rolling into a tight tube.

INSTRUCTIONS

Roll a ping-pong-size ball (about 1½ in [4 cm]) of Table Tortilla Masa (page 114) or Frying Tortilla Masa (page 132) and press into a tortilla. I prefer to first cook the tortilla as I would a Table Tortilla (page 119) to ensure that the tortilla is soft and can easily be rolled later on without cracking.

After searing both sides (and, if possible, achieving a puff), remove from the heat and let cool to room temperature.

To assemble, top each tortilla with your choice of filling, positioned close to one edge and evenly covering about one-third of the tortilla surface. Starting from the filled side, roll the tortilla into a cigar shape and insert a toothpick to keep it rolled up.

Heat 2 in [5 cm] of oil to 350°F [180°C] and fry the flautas until golden brown and crispy, about 2 minutes. (They can also be pan-fried in enough oil to cover the bottom of the pan.) Remove the toothpick before serving. These are best served warm.

Storage: Flautas are best enjoyed immediately, but I'm not above eating them the next day (or second day, or seventh) if refrigerated. Uncooked, they can be frozen for up to 1 year or refrigerated for up to 7 days.

Gordita

A thick tortilla turned masa pocket, usually larger in diameter than an arepa (page 155) but not necessarily thicker

ROOTS: Mexico

FORMAT: Stuffer

COOKING METHOD: Comal, fried

Gorditas are common throughout central and northern Mexico, including Michoacán, Querétaro, Veracruz, Tlaxcala, and Guanajuato. There's a deep-fried version wherein the masa is first stuffed (often with chicharrón), then fried, and finally scored with a single slit in order to add salsa before serving. Querétaro has a version called empedrados de alverjón, a gordita with toasted peas mixed into the masa. Sometimes *gordita* can refer to a large, thick sope (page 199), or even a cake that can be both sweet and savory. There are also triangular gorditas known as tlaxcales, made with partially crushed (*martajado*) nixtamal, sugar, and cinnamon, as well as the itacates (also triangular) from Morelos.

INSTRUCTIONS

Preheat the comal to medium-high heat. Roll a racquetball-size ball (about 2 in [5 cm]) of Table Tortilla Masa (page 114). Using your hands, flatten into a ¼ in [6 mm] thick pancake.

Lower the comal to medium heat. Cook one side of the gordita for about 3 minutes. A nice, lightly colored crust should start to form on the cooked side. Flip the gordita to the uncooked side and cook for another 3 minutes. Continue cooking on each side for another minute or so, each, until cooked through the center. To avoid overcooking the gordita's exterior, you can also finish the last bit of cooking (2 to 4 minutes) in the oven preheated to 400°F [200°C]. A soft, cooked, molten center is the goal.

Remove from the heat and let cool for 5 minutes. While the gordita's still warm, use the tip of a paring knife to cut a horizontal slit through the top. Holding the sides of the gordita with one hand, gently work the middle three fingers of your other hand through the slit and wiggle your fingers to open the pocket for stuffing.

Fill the inside with any stuffing you'd like, whether stewed meats, cheeses, or vegetables. These are best served warm.

Storage: Gorditas (without filling) should keep for up to 7 days in your refrigerator or 1 year frozen. Prior to reheating on a comal, a little bit of water rubbed on either side of the gordita will help replenish any moisture lost during storage.

Hard-Shell Taco

A U-shaped fried tortilla

ROOTS: Mexico (yes, Mexico)

FORMAT: Topper

COOKING METHOD: Deep-fried

Confusingly, like flautas/taquitos (page 169), hard-shell tacos are also called *tacos dorados* ("golden tacos"). That name, of course, refers to the color the tortillas develop when fried, not the shape.

Much to the surprise of most who consider hard-shell tacos to be inauthentic or uniquely American in origin, hard taco shells were most likely conceived in Mexico, introduced by Mexicans to the United States, and ultimately commoditized by Taco Bell.

A similar, albeit less established version of this dish, called a *jonuco*, can be found in the Mexican state of Hidalgo. It consists of two chile-guajillo-bathed table tortillas stuffed with shredded chicken and deep-fried to a crisp.

While a table tortilla—preferably one that has dried out a bit—is ideal for creating a hard-shell taco, a frying tortilla is, in fact, more "authentic" to the Taco Bell version that made this dish famous.

A baked hard-shell is perfectly acceptable (bake in the oven preheated to 375°F [190°C] for about 10 minutes, directly draped over the metal racks), but it will lack the snappy crispness that the original fried version yields.

As for fillings, you know the drill: ground beef, shredded yellow Cheddar cheese, chopped tomatoes, sour cream, taco sauce . . .

INSTRUCTIONS

Prepare the Frying Tortilla (page 135) one of two ways:

→ Option 1 (preferred): Dry at room temperature on the counter for at least 1 hour.

→ Option 2 (faster): Preheat the oven to 350°F [180°C] and heat the tortilla for 5 minutes on a sheet pan with a grill rack.

Heat 1 in [2.5 cm] of oil to 375°F [190°C] and deep-fry the prepared tortilla for 10 to 15 seconds and then flip over, using tongs. Once flipped, carefully fold the tortilla in half and hold with the tongs for another 15 seconds. Continue cooking until the shell is golden brown and/or crispy.

Transfer the shell from the oil to a folded paper towel to drain any excess oil. If seasoning, do so immediately with finely ground salt. These are best served warm.

Storage: When stored properly in an airtight container or freezer bag, hard taco shells may be cooked ahead of time and later reheated in the oven. Ideal storage times vary, but 1 week is my suggested maximum, to avoid staleness.

THE HARD-SHELL TACO

I was surprised to learn that hard-shell tacos were the first kind of taco consumed across the United States. Originally stuffed with more humble cuts of offal meat, the hard-shell taco evolved with the times in America. As the children of late nineteenth- and early twentieth-century Mexican immigrants started to advance economically, they increasingly adapted their ingredients to reflect the more commercially available ingredients of the US larder, like hamburger meat, Cheddar cheese, and iceberg lettuce. The hard-shell taco is therefore not the bastardization of the taco many of us assume, but a distinctly Mexican adaptation of the staple, adjusted for local context.

Further, contrary to popular sentiment, Taco Bell did not invent the hard-shell taco, nor did it technically first conceive of the frying technology that it developed for preparing hard-shell tacos more efficiently. While no single person can be credited with "inventing" the hard taco shell, experts agree that its genesis occurred in Mexico. Glen Bell, the late founder of Taco Bell, was inspired by a Mexican restaurant in San Bernardino called Mitla Café, whose hard-shell tacos were popular with the local Mexican community. As for the hard-shell frying technology that Bell claimed to have pioneered in the 1960s, the first hard-shell-taco-frying patent on record was actually registered in 1947 by Juvencio Maldonado, a Oaxacan restaurant owner living in New York. And even before Juvencio Maldonado, in the late 1930s, George Ashley of Absolute Mexican Food started selling tortillas and taco molds for preparing hard-shell tacos at home.

Huarache

An oblong masa pancake

ROOTS: Mexico

FORMAT: Always a topper, sometimes also a stuffer

COOKING METHOD: Comal, fried

This shape gets its name from the woven sandals commonly worn throughout Mexico, known as *huaraches* (the same sandal from which Nike derived the name and inspiration for one of its best-selling shoes). These edible huaraches are typically large-format dishes (think US men's size 12), which, while sometimes shared, are often enjoyed topped with meat as a main course. Smaller versions are, of course, also welcome. Some styles of huaraches, like those in Mexico City, may be stuffed with refried beans before being griddled on the comal or plancha, like a giant tlacoyo (page 205). In nearby Toluca, huaraches dorados are prepared with *maíz quebrado* (broken corn) and served crispy like a cracker. Others, like some prepared throughout Oaxaca, aren't stuffed but instead topped with beans and other condiments.

It is also not uncommon to find huaraches that are precooked on the comal and finished in the fryer.

INSTRUCTIONS

We've assumed a comal-prepared, larger-format main-course version here, but feel free to scale down as you see fit.

Preheat the comal to medium-high heat. Roll a racquetball-size ball (2 in [5 cm]) of Table Tortilla Masa (page 114) and shape into a 10 to 12 in [25 to 30 cm] log. You can then flatten with a tortilla press, if you have one that is large enough, or a huarache press (they exist!), but it's often easier to place the masa log between two sheets of plastic wrap on the countertop and flatten with either your hands and/or some kind of rolling pin (such as the side of a wine bottle). Aim for about ⅛ in [3 mm] thickness. Note that well-hydrated masa makes the pressing much easier, especially when using the countertop method.

Lower the comal to medium heat. Cook one side of the huarache for about 3 minutes. Flip over and let the second side cook for another 3 minutes. Continue flipping and cooking until cooked through to the center. As with tlacoyos (page 205), I like a texture contrast between a crusty exterior and soft center. Enjoy immediately, or if planning to use within the next 6 to 12 hours, let rest wrapped in a kitchen towel at room temperature. These are best served warm.

Storage: Cooked huaraches (without toppings) can be stored for up to 7 days in the refrigerator or 1 year frozen. A little bit of water rubbed on either side of the huarache will help replenish any moisture lost during storage, prior to reheating with a comal.

Infladita

A crispy tortilla puff with a hollow interior, meant for stuffing and topping

ROOTS: Mexico (especially Veracruz)

FORMAT: Stuffer, topper

COOKING METHOD: Deep-fried

These are reminiscent of Indian puri (poori), the fried, puffed, wheat-flour based flatbread of India. In Veracruz, their full name is *gorditas infladas* ("puffy chubbies"), often "gorditas," for short.

INSTRUCTIONS

Roll a 1 in [2.5 cm] ball of masa and press to a table tortilla thinness (see page 119).

Heat 1 to 2 in [2.5 to 5 cm] of oil to 375°F [190°C]. Roll a ¾ in [2 cm] ball of Table Tortilla Masa (page 114) and press it to a table tortilla thinness (see page 119). Over medium-high heat, sear each side of the tortilla for 10 seconds on a comal.

Remove the small tortilla from the comal and drop it into the preheated oil; it will begin to puff almost immediately. After 30 seconds, gently flip the tortilla and spoon hot oil onto the exposed face to ensure even, golden-brown coloring and cooking through the outside. Fry in the oil for 30 to 60 seconds total, until golden brown. The infladita should be puffy and crisp but not quite brittle.

Using a slotted spoon or spider, transfer to a folded paper towel to drain the remaining oil. While still hot, season with fine sea salt (optional).

Let cool for 30 to 60 seconds, then use the tip of a paring knife to cut a 1 in [2.5 cm] hole through the top layer of the tortilla—ideally in the thinner of the two sides. This way, the thicker bottom layer can absorb any juices or oils from the topping without breaking.

When ready to serve, stuff the infladita through the opening and top with any garnishes. If stuffed too far in advance, the texture will become soggy and cause the infladita to fall apart.

Storage: Infladitas can hold for an hour or so before going stale. They don't store particularly well in an airtight container, but this may buy you a few more hours of quality texture before they begin to degrade.

Memela

A thick tortilla with subtle indentations for holding salsas and toppings; can be *pretty* close to a sope (page 199), but with less-defined ridges

ROOTS: Mexico (Oaxaca)

FORMAT: Topper

COOKING METHOD: Comal

While delicious on any occasion, for me, memelas are the breakfast of champions. A little asiento (page 218), bean purée, queso fresco, and salsa: success.

INSTRUCTIONS

Preheat the comal to medium-high heat. Roll a ping-pong-size ball (about 1½ in [4 cm]) of Table Tortilla Masa (page 114). Following the same process as for a Table Tortilla (page 119), apply light pressure to your press to make a tortilla about ⅛ in [3 mm] thick. You can also shape them by hand, if you find your tortilla press is giving you a thinner memela than you'd like. In this case, place the masa ball between plastic liners of your tortilla press and pat the plastic down with your hand until you reach your desired thickness.

Carefully remove the uncooked memela from the plastic liner.

Lower the comal to medium heat. Cook one side of the memela for about 60 seconds, yielding a light, gentle sear. Flip and cook the second side for another 60 seconds. With the flat tip of your index finger (wrapped in a kitchen towel, if you like, to prevent burning your finger), make subtle indentations across the surface of the memela. Flip back to the first seared side and cook for another 30 seconds. Some puffing may occur, though pliability is less critical here than for a table tortilla.

Before removing from the comal, top the memela (indentation side up) with any fats or cheeses, so that they slightly sizzle and melt. These are best served warm.

Storage: A fresh memela is best enjoyed immediately, but can be stored (without toppings) for up to 7 days refrigerated or 1 year frozen. A little bit of water rubbed on either side of the memela will help replenish any moisture lost during storage, prior to reheating with a comal.

Molote

A torpedo-shaped fritter, typically stuffed with ground beef or chorizo

ROOTS: Mexico (Oaxaca, Puebla, Yucatán)
FORMAT: Always a stuffer, sometimes also a topper
COOKING METHOD: Deep-fried

Some versions are topped with a loose black bean purée, avocado crema, cheese, and lettuce or cabbage; others are eaten naked. I prefer molotes topped with all of the condiments, please. A similar Yucatecan version traditionally filled with beans, pepitas, and herbs, shaped like a snake's head, is called *polkan* (from the Mayan word for "snake head"). Despite my best attempts, my precooking molotes sometimes come out more like polkanes—looking more like a snake's head than a torpedo—but it all works out in the fryer. In some parts of Mexico, *molotes* refer to empanada-shaped, stuffed half-moons of masa. Some variations incorporate mashed potato into the masa before shaping, which is similar to one of my favorite Cuban snacks, papas rellenas.

INSTRUCTIONS

I've seen recipes call for pressing a tortilla first, then filling and folding (like my tlacoyo hack, see page 205), but I think it's easiest to approach this like a chochoyote (page 165) or a bollo (page 159). This way, you get a thicker-set torpedo instead of a uniform log shape.

To begin, roll a ping-pong-size ball (about 1½ in [4 cm]) of Table Tortilla Masa (page 114). Press your fingertip into the center, creating an indentation about a third to halfway into the ball. Gently pack your stuffing into the crater, taking care to not mound up above the edge of the opening. With moist hands, gradually sculpt the edges over the stuffing, enclosing it in the center of what should again look like a ball. Continue to sculpt into a stout torpedo shape. Place on a baking sheet and cover with a damp kitchen towel until ready for frying.

Heat 2 in [5 cm] of oil to 350°F [180°C]. Carefully add a few molotes at a time (as space allows), taking care to not crowd them in the oil, as the temperature will decrease with each uncooked molote added and result in a greasier finish. Fry for about 4 minutes, or until golden brown outside.

Using a slotted spoon or spider, transfer to paper towels to drain the remaining oil. While still hot, season with salt (optional) and serve immediately.

Storage: A fried molote is best enjoyed immediately, while hot, and does not store well. You can store uncooked molotes in the refrigerator for up to 3 days or in the freezer for up to 1 year.

Panucho

A stuffed, fried tostada

ROOTS: Mexico (Yucatán), Belize

FORMAT: Stuffer and topper

COOKING METHOD: Comal, fried

You need a table tortilla that puffs for this dish, as the puff creates the cavity wherein you will stuff your fillings. It is also easiest to handle and cut the tortilla open while still warm off the comal.

Traditionally found in Yucatán, panuchos are stuffed with refried black beans and hardboiled egg, and topped with meat like pork (cochinita pibil) or chicken.

INSTRUCTIONS

Begin by assembling, pressing, and cooking a Table Tortilla (page 119), ideally about 4 in [10 cm] in diameter. Once it puffs, let it cool slightly (about 5 minutes), then cut a horizontal slit through the top layer of the tortilla, carefully separating the top layer from the bottom. Spread filling (room-temperature refried beans are an excellent choice) evenly on the inside of the tortilla.

Heat 2 in [5 cm] of oil, or enough to completely submerge the filled tortilla, to 350°F [180°C]. Fry each filled tortilla until golden brown, about 2 minutes, and transfer to a folded paper towel to drain. These are best served warm. Top with any combination of condiments.

Storage: Panuchos are best enjoyed immediately, but, as with flautas (page 169), I'm not above eating them the next day (or second day, or seventh) if refrigerated. In this case, I'll gladly eat them cold, room temp, or bake them at 375°F [190°C] for 5 minutes in the oven until warmed through. Uncooked, they do not store well in either refrigerator or freezer, as the filling will ultimately lead to sogginess.

Puffy Taco

Part salbut (page 195), part infladita (page 179), part tostada (page 213), all in the name of taco

ROOTS: USA (San Antonio, TX)

FORMAT: Topper

COOKING METHOD: Fried

Given its provenance, the puffy taco may feel inauthentic to some, despite the fact that Mexicans living in the United States created it. Those who mock this phenomenon, however, are sadly missing out. Fill it with whatever "authentic" ingredients you'd like—could be a chicken tinga, or go for broke with a Taco Bell–style ground beef. Whatever you do, this taco shell is masa manna for the soul.

INSTRUCTIONS

Roll a ping-pong-size ball (1½ in [4 cm]) of Table Tortilla Masa (page 114) and press into a thick table tortilla about ⅛ in [3 mm] thick. Because of how much the tortilla expands—creating thin, crispy "skins" that are prone to breaking—I find it helpful sometimes to press it a little thicker rather than thinner, so that it all holds together better when topped as a taco. Adjust the thickness to your preference.

Heat 2 in [5 cm] of oil to 375°F [190°C]. Add the uncooked, pressed tortilla; it will begin to puff almost immediately. Once it has, flip it over and let the other side cook for about 5 seconds before folding the tortilla at a roughly 45-degree angle. You can do this by lightly pinning the tortilla down with the side of your spider/slotted spoon and carefully folding one half of the tortilla over. Hold the position for 5 to 10 seconds,

until the shape has taken hold. Gently flip the now-folded taco shell over every 5 seconds and carefully spoon or baste hot oil over it to ensure even coloring and cooking through the outside. About 30 seconds total in the oil should be sufficient. The taco shell should be puffy, crisp, and golden brown.

Using a slotted spoon or spider, transfer the taco shell to a folded paper towel to drain the remaining oil. While still hot, season with salt (optional).

Fill or top the puffy taco shell right before serving, otherwise the texture will become soggy. These are best served warm.

Storage: Puffy taco shells can hold for an hour or so before going stale. They don't store particularly well in an airtight container, but this may buy you a few more hours of quality texture before it begins to degrade.

Pupusa

A stuffed masa pancake with toppings

ROOTS: El Salvador, Honduras

FORMAT: Stuffer and topper

COOKING METHOD: Comal

Translated from Pipil language as "swollen," pupusas are a lot like gorditas (page 171) in some respects, but they are so iconic, they deserved their own shape. They're most often filled with some combination of refried beans and shredded, low-moisture melting cheese (a mozzarella could work, for example) and topped with a lightly fermented relish (curtido) and salsa.

A lesser-known masa shape from Puebla called *pintos*, and *bocoles* (sometimes called *bocoles pintos*) from Hidalgo, are prepared in much the same way as pupusas, but use whole cooked beans mixed directly into the masa.

Like chochoyotes (page 165) or bollos (page 159), pupusas will often incorporate a bit of fat and salt into the masa, but this part is totally up to you. If using fat, like vegetable oil, I recommend beginning with 10 percent fat weight of total masa weight (1:10 ratio). If you plan to shape and then immediately freeze them, a bit of fat mixed into the masa will help preserve the integrity of the pupusas through the eventual thaw. I enjoy them both with and without the additional fat and find that the fillings have more than enough salt for my taste.

INSTRUCTIONS

Preheat the comal to medium-high heat. Roll a ping-pong-size ball (about 1½ in [4 cm]) of Table Tortilla Masa (page 114).

Press your fingertip into the center, creating an indentation about a third to halfway into the ball. Gently pack your stuffing into the crater, taking care not to mound up above the edge of the opening. With moist hands, gradually sculpt the edges over the stuffing, enclosing it in the center of what should again look like a ball. Flatten the ball into a pancake about ¼ in [6 mm] thick, taking care to not tear the masa and expose the filling.

Lower the comal to medium heat. Cook one side of the pupusa for about 3 minutes. A nice crust should start to form on the cooked side, with light coloring. Flip the pupusa to the uncooked side and cook for another 3 minutes. Continue cooking for another minute or so on each side until cooked through the center. To avoid overcooking the pupusa's exterior, you can also finish the last bit of cooking (5 to 10 minutes) in the oven preheated to 400°F [200°C]. These are best served warm.

Storage: A fresh pupusa is best enjoyed immediately, but can be stored (without toppings) for up to 7 days refrigerated or 1 year frozen. A little bit of water rubbed on either side of the pupusa will help replenish any moisture lost during storage, prior to reheating on a comal.

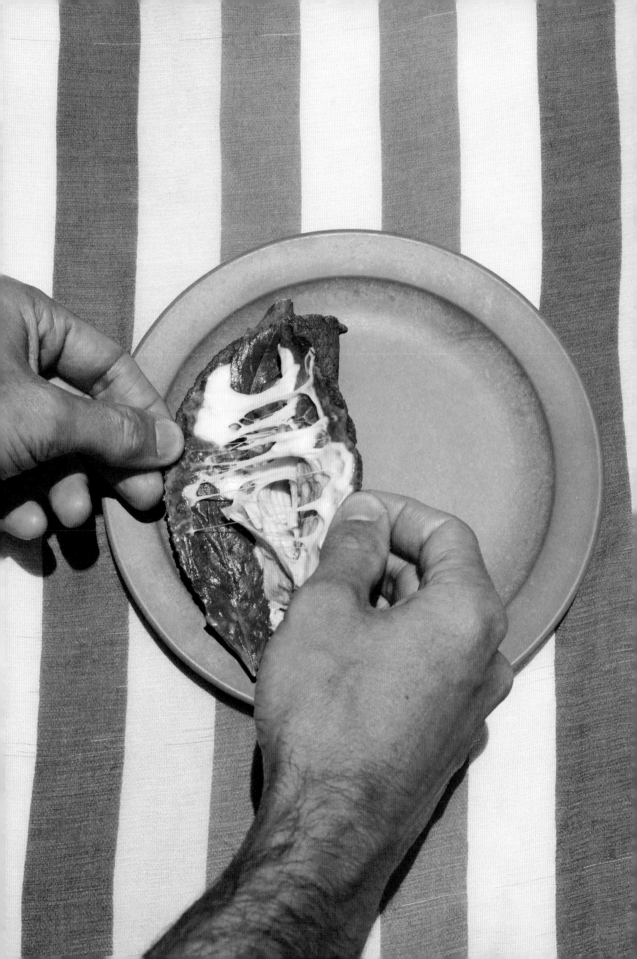

Quesadilla (Comal)

A folded table tortilla stuffed with cheese or other fillings

ROOTS: Mexico

FORMAT: Stuffer and topper

COOKING METHOD: Comal

Throughout Mexico, quesadillas do not necessarily *have* to have cheese in order to be called a quesadilla. Think of them as a foldover taco, a blank slate for incorporating a range of fillings, which can include but are not limited to cheese. If cheese is a prerequisite for you, when ordering at an establishment you'll want to be sure to expressly request it, along with any of its other common fillings—for example, flor de calabaza (squash blossoms), epazote, or huitlacoche.

As for size, the street-side quesadillas you'll find in Mexico are usually quite large, with what's about a 10 in [25 cm] tortilla base, on average. ("Machetes" are an even larger variation on this theme.) High-fat, low-moisture Oaxacan cheese will always be the pinnacle of cheeses in this application, but a low-moisture mozzarella or Muenster will also yield fine results.

Side note: A quesadilla filled with fish, without cheese, is called a *pescadilla*.

INSTRUCTIONS

Preheat the comal to medium-high heat. Roll a 2 in [5 cm] ball of Table Tortilla Masa (page 114) and press it into a tortilla. I prefer to cook the tortilla as I would a Table Tortilla (page 119) to ensure that the tortilla is soft and can easily be folded in half without cracking. After you have seared both sides (and, if possible, achieved a puff), top one half of the tortilla with cheese and/or whatever fillings you'd like. Fold the tortilla in half and lightly press down with your fingers or a spatula, so that it remains folded. I like to continue cooking until a bit of color is developed on both sides of the quesadilla and the cheese (if using) is fully melted.

Storage: Quesadillas are best enjoyed immediately, but, like a handful of other masa shapes, I'm not above eating them the next day (or second day, or third) if refrigerated. You can freeze uncooked quesadillas for up to 1 year or refrigerate for up to 3 days.

Quesadilla (Fried)

Fried masa turnovers stuffed with quesillo (Oaxacan-style string cheese)

ROOTS: Mexico

FORMAT: Stuffer and topper

COOKING METHOD: Deep-fried

These are basically cheese empanadas, but if you were to call them that in Mexico, you might get confused looks.

Like many fried foods in Mexico, quesadillas are often fried in lard. While this is a delicious choice, any kind of frying oil will do.

INSTRUCTIONS

Roll a 2 in [5 cm] ball of Table Tortilla Masa (page 114) or Frying Tortilla Masa (page 135) and press into a thick tortilla (about ⅛ in [3 mm] thick). Remove the top plastic liner and load cheese into the center of the tortilla, leaving room along the edges for a clean seal. Pack with enough cheese to ensure an even, hearty filling, but take care to not overdo it—you want to be able to neatly fold the quesadilla without rupturing. Lightly wet the outer edges of the tortilla to seal.

Lift the edge of the bottom plastic liner to support one half of the tortilla as you fold it over the filling to form a half moon–shaped turnover. Use your fingers or the tines of a fork to gently press and seal the edges, ensuring that the filling is securely packed inside.

Heat 3 in [7.5 cm] of oil to 350°F [180°C]. Fry the quesadilla until golden brown and crispy, about 3 minutes. Serve naked or with salsa (a raw salsa verde is an excellent choice), guacamole crema, refried black beans, iceberg lettuce, or shredded cabbage and even queso fresco.

Storage: Quesadillas are best enjoyed immediately, but, as with a handful of other masa shapes, I'm not above eating them the next day (or second day, or third) if refrigerated. You can freeze uncooked quesadillas for up to 1 year or refrigerate for up to 3 days.

Salbut

A variation on the tostada (page 213), albeit more puffed and chewy than crisp and brittle

ROOTS: **Mexico (Yucatán), Belize**

FORMAT: **Topper**

COOKING METHOD: **Fried**

Salbut is derived from the Mayan words *zaal*, meaning "light" and *but*, meaning "stuffed." These are often served with shredded chicken or turkey, avocados, pickled onions, and habanero salsa.

INSTRUCTIONS

Roll a 1 in [2.5 cm] ball of Table Tortilla Masa (page 114) and press into a 4 in [10 cm] table tortilla (about 1/16 in [1.5 mm] thick).

Heat 1 to 2 in [2.5 to 5 cm] of oil to 350°F [180°C]. Add the tortilla; it will begin to puff almost immediately. After 30 seconds, gently flip the tortilla and carefully spoon hot oil onto the exposed face to ensure even coloring and cooking through the outside. Continue to cook for another 30 seconds, or until puffy and crisp.

Using a slotted spoon or spider, transfer the salbut to a folded paper towel to drain. While still hot, immediately blot each salbut with another paper towel, pressing down on the puff to depress and create a crater in its surface. The tortilla should be cooked enough to still be a bit flexible while hot, which should allow it to give when pressed on without entirely falling apart. Season with salt while hot.

Top right before serving, otherwise the texture will become soggy. These are best served warm.

Storage: Salbutes can hold for an hour or so before going stale. They don't store particularly well in an airtight container, but it may buy you a few more hours of quality texture before it begins to degrade.

Soft-Shell Taco

A soft, pliable, wrappable, edible plate

ROOTS: Mexico

FORMAT: Topper

COOKING METHOD: Comal

A.k.a. table tortilla, blandita, or simply tortilla. Perhaps the most ubiquitous masa shape in all the world.

The literal translation of *tortilla* is "little tart," a diminutive of the Spanish *torta*, or "round cake," though the Nahuatl word for tortilla is *tlaxcalli*. However, the masa shape and name *taco* that we know today is believed to have originated around the eighteenth century in, of all places, the Mexican silver-mining community. These miners used "tacos" to refer to the explosives that they used for ore excavation—little charges of gunpowder hand-wrapped in pieces of paper. Historian Jeffrey Pilcher suggests that an edible taco (especially a tightly rolled taco of the flauta/taquito persuasion) topped with red salsa or hot sauce bears an uncanny resemblance to a stick of dynamite.

Although the word *taco* doesn't appear as a dish name until the late nineteenth century, tacos have arguably existed for as long as tortillas (let's say a few thousand years, in some form or another).

Of course, a table tortilla can be used for far more than just tacos: think enchiladas, enfrijoladas, enmoladas, totopos, and tostadas, to name a few. They are even burned and ground into a coffee, like in Chiapas, or ground and reused in fresh masa.

INSTRUCTIONS
See the Table Tortilla recipe on page 119.

Sope

A thick masa pancake, often with a raised ridge for retaining toppings

ROOTS: Mexico (Central/Southern Mexico: Guerrero, Estado de México, Oaxaca, Puebla, etc.), Guatemala

FORMAT: Topper

COOKING METHOD: Comal and/or fried

Sopes are also known as pellizcada, picadita, and garnacha (Yucatán and Guatemala). Any size sope goes, really, but they're often 3 to 4 in [7.5 to 10 cm] across and enjoyed as an antojito ("little whim") or appetizer. In the Yucatán, the sopes (garnachas) may have a higher ridge, more closely resembling small cups.

INSTRUCTIONS

Comal: Preheat the comal to medium-high heat. Roll a ping-pong-size ball (about 1½ in [4 cm]) of Table Tortilla Masa (page 114). You can flatten with a tortilla press, but it's far more fun (and I think easier) to use your hands to shape the sope into a ¼ to ½ in [6 to 12 mm] thick pancake. You can do this either freehand, or by flattening a masa ball onto a flat surface (like your kitchen counter) with your palm, and then use the counter to maintain a flat bottom.

Lower the comal to medium heat. Cook one side of the sope for about 2 minutes. Flip over and let the second side cook for another 2 to 3 minutes. While the second side cooks and the first cooked side is still quite soft, pinch the edges to create a short ridge around the circumference to retain sauces and additional toppings. (You may also remove the sopes after each side

has cooked for 2 minutes, if you'd prefer not to create the rim while the sope is in the pan. Alternatively, you can try shaping the sope and creating its ridge before you place it on the comal.) Flip the sope back to the ridged side for another 2 to 3 minutes. Continue cooking until cooked through to the center, but still soft. Enjoy immediately, or if you plan to use it within the next 6 to 12 hours, let rest wrapped in a kitchen towel at room temperature.

Fried: For best results, parcook the sope on the comal for 1 to 2 minutes per side. The reduced moisture from parcooking prevents bubbling and allows for a crispier finish on the outside. Heat 2 in [5 cm] of oil to 350°F [180°C]. Add the sope and fry for 2 minutes, or until golden brown. Remove with a slotted spoon or spider and place on paper towels to drain excess oil. These are best served warm.

Storage: A fresh comal-prepared sope is best enjoyed immediately, but may be stored (without toppings) for up to 7 days refrigerated or 1 year frozen. A little bit of water rubbed on either side of the sope will help replenish any moisture lost during storage, prior to reheating with a comal. A fried sope should be enjoyed immediately; they do not store well.

Tamal

Wrapped masa cakes

ROOTS: Mesoamerica, South America, Caribbean

FORMAT: Stuffer, topper

COOKING METHOD: Steamed, comal, sometimes grilled

The word *tamale* is derived from the Nahuatl *tamalli*, which means "unformed corn dough." This being a ubiquitous staple across Latin America, the basic tamal recipe has led to endless variations.

INSTRUCTIONS
See Masa for Tamales on page 142.

Tetela

A stuffed, sealed triangular envelope that loosely resembles a small crêpe

ROOTS: Mexico

FORMAT: Stuffer and topper

COOKING METHOD: Comal

The word *tetela* is a combination of the Nahuatl words *tetl* ("hill") and *tla* ("many"), which translates as "place of many hills." There are several towns throughout Mexico bearing this name—such as Tetela (Oaxaca), Tetela de Ocampo (Puebla), and Tetela del Volcán (Morelos)—where hills and mountains indeed mark the landscape, but where the eponymous dish is notably absent. All accounts seem to indicate that tetelas originated somewhere in Oaxaca, specifically in the Mixteca region, though they are also served in Puebla by the name *memelas*. The tetela name is most likely a reference to the tetela's peaked, triangular shape, which bears resemblance to a one-dimensionally drawn symbol for *mountain*.

Tetelas can be filled with just about anything, but most commonly with refried beans and topped with crema, queso fresco, and/or salsa.

INSTRUCTIONS

Preheat the comal to medium-high heat. Roll a ping-pong-size ball (about 1½ in [4 cm]) of Table Tortilla Masa (page 114). Following instructions for a Table Tortilla (page 119), press the ball into a tortilla, remove the top plastic liner, and spread a bit of filling across the center. To shape the tetela, with the plastic liner squared as you face the tortilla, lift the top right corner of

cont'd

the plastic and fold it with the right edge of the tortilla to a 45-degree angle, creating a pointed tip at the top of the tortilla. Repeat on the left side. Finally, grasp the lower center of the plastic liner and fold the remaining flap over to create a well-defined, straight-edged triangle.

There should be little to no exposure of the filling through the seams, ensuring that the contents are well enclosed.

Lower the comal to medium heat. Place the tetela seam-side up on the comal. Cook for 4 to 6 minutes per side, until cooked through the center with a slight char on each side. You can test for doneness with a cake tester, if you'd like, though I prefer testing by feel. When pressed down, the tetela shouldn't give or bounce much—it should feel like a well-done steak, indicating a dense interior. As with a tlacoyo (page 205), I love a tetela with a chewy, crispy crust (sometimes called *bark*) with a contrasting molten center.
No extra fat is needed to cook a tetela, but a little bit applied directly to the tetela toward the last minute of cooking is never something I regret. I'll use whatever I have around, from bacon fat to schmaltz to ghee. These are best served warm.

Storage: A fresh-cooked tetela is best enjoyed immediately, but can be stored (without toppings) for up to 7 days refrigerated or 1 year frozen. A little bit of water rubbed on either side of the tetela will help replenish any moisture lost during storage, prior to reheating on a comal.

Tlacoyo

A football-shaped or oval masa pocket, commonly filled with puréed beans, favas, or other pulses and topped with cheese, crema, salsa, and/or onions with cilantro; looks like a diminutive, stuffed huarache (page 177)

ROOTS: Mexico (Estado de México, Hidalgo, Puebla)

FORMAT: Stuffer and topper

COOKING METHOD: Comal or fried

I love a chewy, crispy crust (sometimes called *bark*) with a contrasting molten center. Traditionally, lard is incorporated into the masa to achieve this texture. While that's delicious, I don't find it necessary. If using fat, like asiento (page 218) or vegetable oil, I recommend beginning with 10 percent fat weight of total masa weight (1:10 ratio). If you plan to shape and then immediately freeze tlacoyos, a bit of fat mixed into the masa will help preserve their integrity through the eventual thaw. And if you do incorporate fat, note that it will darken the color of the masa when cooked.

INSTRUCTIONS

Many pros in Mexico can shape these entirely by hand; others may use a tortilla press so expertly that they can flatten the filled masa into perfect, oval-shaped submission. I am particularly inept at shaping most doughs, so I do a hybrid press-and-fold approach.

Comal: Preheat the comal to medium-high heat. Roll a ping-pong-size ball (about 1½ in [4 cm]) of Table Tortilla Masa (page 114). Press into a tortilla, remove the top plastic liner, and spread a bit of filling across the center.

To shape the tlacoyo, lift the bottom plastic liner to fold the left side of the tortilla

cont'd

halfway across itself. Repeat on the right side. You should now have a somewhat symmetrical, partially closed rectangular-shaped taco of sorts. Again using the bottom plastic liner, fold the upper corners over, creating a somewhat pointed tip on both ends. At this point, I slightly flatten the seams enough to ensure that they don't burst open during cooking—but not too much, because I kinda like the complexity of texture that they add.

Lower the comal to medium heat. Place the tlacoyo seam-side up on the comal. Cook for 4 to 6 minutes per side, until cooked through the center with a slight char on each side. You can test for doneness with a cake tester if you'd like, though I prefer testing by feel. When pressed down, the tlacoyo shouldn't give or bounce much—it should feel like a well-done steak, indicating a dense interior. No fat is needed, but a little bit applied directly to the tlacoyo toward the last minute of cooking is never something I regret. I'll use whatever I have around, from bacon fat to schmaltz to ghee. These are best served warm.

Fried: For best results, parcook the tlacoyo on the comal for 1 to 2 minutes per side. The reduced moisture prevents bubbling and ruptures and allows for a crispier finish on the exterior. Heat 2 in [5 cm] of oil to 350°F [180°C] and deep-fry the tlacoyo for 3 to 4 minutes, or until golden brown. It should be crisp on the outside and moist, molten, and steamy on the inside.

Storage: A fresh comal-prepared tlacoyo is best enjoyed immediately, but may be stored (without toppings) for up to 7 days refrigerated or 1 year frozen. A little bit of water rubbed on either side of the tlacoyo will help replenish any moisture lost during storage, prior to reheating with a comal.

Tlayuda

A large-format, burrito-size (12 to 14 in [30 to 35 cm]) tortilla that is often crisped, topped, and served open-faced (pizza style) or folded over (calzone style)

ROOTS: Mexico (Oaxaca)

FORMAT: Topper

COOKING METHOD: Comal

Tlayudas are sometimes called *clayudas*, as the latter is considered easier to pronounce in English-speaking contexts.

These large-format tortillas appear in three distinct textures; however, only one of the three is technically called a *tlayuda*. That's because the name itself refers to a specific level of cooking doneness of the tortilla:

→ A fresh tlayuda with the consistency of a table tortilla is called a *blanda*. These are still moist and pliable, perfect for tearing off pieces to accompany each bite of food at mealtime.

→ The semi-toasted version is called a *tlayuda*. This is my personal favorite, ideal for folding and crisping up later on with asiento (page 218)/fat, black bean purée, quesillo, thinly-sliced cabbage, and salsa tucked inside.

→ A fully-toasted tlayuda is referred to as a *tostada* or, in some cases, a *totopo*. It's an enormous, crunchy, baked masa cracker that often accompanies salsas and soups. adding a satisfying textural contrast.

The structural integrity of tortillas of this size is supported by the bolita corn varietal, found throughout the Valles Centrales of Oaxaca. When preparing masa for tlayudas, some producers will traditionally nixtamalize this corn in ash instead of cal.

INSTRUCTIONS

We'll assume the semi-toasted route here. You can adjust the cooking time up or down for either of the other two options.

To cook a tortilla of the traditional tlayuda size requires a larger comal than many home cooks have on hand. A full-size (20 in [50 cm] or larger) comal or professional plancha will do the trick, or you can also scale the size down to your needs and liking. You can find a tlayuda-size tortilla press online (see page 250).

Preheat the comal to medium-high heat. To prepare a full-size tlayuda, roll a tennis-ball-size ball (about 2½ in [6 cm]) of Table Tortilla Masa (page 114). Following the same process as for a Table Tortilla (page 119), press as if you were preparing a slightly thicker table tortilla (about ⅛ in [3 mm] thick).

Lower the comal to medium heat. Carefully remove the top plastic wrap sheet and drape the tlayuda over the length of your forearm. In a sweeping, backhanded motion, place the uncooked tlayuda on the comal. Cook one side of the tlayuda for about 60 seconds. Flip and cook the second side for another 60 seconds. Flipping

cont'd

back and forth, cook until the tlayuda is firm but still pliable, about 7 minutes total. You can use a metal trivet on your comal to prevent burning, and you can also occasionally mist water over the tlayuda if you find it is drying out too fast. The goal is to eventually fold it over without its breaking in half—it will have a seemingly stale texture. Let cool completely if not using immediately.

To serve, preheat a wood or gas grill on medium-high heat and briefly reheat both sides for 45 to 60 seconds.

Remove and apply fat (traditionally asiento, page 218), beans, and cheese of your choice to one half of the surface. Fold the tlayuda in half without breaking it and return it to the grill, using tongs to keep the fold in place until it crisps and sets in position. If working with open flames, fan them to kiss the tlayuda lightly with color. Repeat on both sides until the tlayuda is crispy, nicely colored, and the fillings have nicely rendered and melted.

Add any additional toppings to the center or top of the tlayuda, such as meat, salsa, and thinly shredded fresh cabbage, as is traditionally served. Enjoy while hot.

Storage: Tlayudas and tostadas can last for several weeks, even months stored at room temperature. A blanda is best enjoyed immediately, but may be stored (without toppings) for up to 7 days refrigerated or 1 year frozen. A little bit of water rubbed on either side of the tlayuda will help replenish any moisture lost during storage, prior to reheating with a comal.

Tostada

A crispy tortilla; tortilla toast

ROOTS: Mesoamerica

FORMAT: Topper

COOKING METHOD: Comal, baked, fried

Tostada means "toasted." As the name suggests, it is a tortilla that is cooked until toasted and crispy. Most tostadas are either fried or toasted on a comal; the exception is the tostadas of Oaxaca's isthmus (totopos, page 215), which are cooked in a tandoori-style oven. The tostada game of Jalisco is especially strong, boasting a homegrown tostada called *raspadas*. These are made by shaving off the top raw layer of a partially cooked tortilla, creating a thin tortilla with one roughly-textured side. The shaved tortilla is then cooked on both sides until dry and crisp.

INSTRUCTIONS

Comal: Preheat the comal to medium-high heat. Roll a ping-pong-size ball (about 1½ in [4 cm]) of Table Tortilla Masa (page 114) and press into a tortilla. Lower the heat to medium. In a sweeping, back-handed motion, place the uncooked tostada on the comal. Cook each side evenly for 1 minute to start. After each side has cooked for 1 minute, allow the tostada to continue cooking until crispy and slightly colored, 2 to 3 more minutes per side. (To prevent charring, you may choose to place a metal trivet between your comal and tostada.)

Baked: Preheat the oven to 375°F [190°C]. It is best (though not essential) to bake tostadas on a baking sheet with a cooling rack. This allows both sides of the tortilla to cook evenly in the oven with well-circulated heat. While oil is optional, I like to coat each side of the Table Tortilla (page 119) with a bit of fat, oil or otherwise, before baking. Bake for about 10 minutes, or until golden brown and crispy. When I've added a bit of oil to these for the bake, I like to season them with salt right out of the oven.

Fried: Frying Tortillas (page 135) or dried-out Table Tortillas (page 119) make for great fried tostadas. As for the latter, you can either leave fresh tortillas sitting out for one hour or lightly dry them in an oven preheated to 350°F [180°C] for 5 minutes. Heat ½ in [13 mm] of oil to 375°F [190°C] and fry the tostadas until golden brown, 30 to 60 seconds. Remove with tongs and place on a folded paper towel to drain any excess oil. Season immediately with salt.

Storage: Tostadas are best enjoyed when fresh; however, they have a longer shelf life at room temperature than table tortillas. When stored properly in an airtight container or freezer bag, tostadas may be kept up to 7 days (if cooked with oil) or even weeks (if toasted on the comal or baked without oil). That said, they may get a bit stale within a week. If so, you can try heating them back up for some additional crisp.

Totopo (Tortilla Chip)

Fried or baked chips

ROOTS: Mexico

FORMAT: Topper

COOKING METHOD: Baked and fried

The word *totopo* comes from the Nahuatl *tlaxcaltotopochtl*, a combination of the words for "tortilla" and "thunder," roughly meaning "tortillas that are noisy to chew."

The most common types of totopos are fried; however, some are indeed baked or cooked on a comal. The totopos of Oaxaca's isthmus region are made using a tandoori-style oven and bear small finger indentations across their surfaces. The *totoposte* of Tabasco (Villahermosa) are made with maíz nuevo, beans, lard, or chicharrón and cooked on a comal.

INSTRUCTIONS

Fried: Cut a Frying Tortilla (page 135) or dried Table Tortilla (page 119) into quarters, fifths, or sixths (strips will also work, if preparing for salad or soup topper). Heat 4 in [10 cm] of oil to 350°F [180°C] and line a baking sheet with paper towels (optional). Test a totopo by dropping it into the fryer; if the oil is hot enough, it should sizzle immediately. When ready, drop the pieces of tortilla into the fryer and move them around somewhat continuously until golden brown, 30 to 60 seconds. With a slotted spoon or spider, remove from the fryer and transfer to the paper towels to let excess oil drain. While still hot, quickly transfer to a mixing bowl. Season with fine sea salt, toss, and serve at once while they are crispy and snappy.

Baked: Preheat the oven to 375°F [190°C]. Cut a Table Tortilla (page 119) into quarters, fifths, or sixths (strips will also work, if preparing for salad or soup topper). Coat the chips lightly with oil (optional) and place as flat and evenly as possible on a full baking sheet (with a cooling rack), ideally not touching one another or the flat surface of the baking sheet so that air can evenly circulate between and around the chips. Bake for 5 minutes, then remove from the oven and flip the chips over. Salt the chips and return to the oven for about 10 more minutes, or until crispy. Oven-baked chips, even with oil, will never be quite as crispy as fried chips, but they'll come close enough while feeling somewhat healthier.

Storage: Totopos are best enjoyed when fresh; however, they have a longer shelf life at room temperature than table tortillas. When stored properly in an airtight container or freezer bag, totopos may be kept up to 7 days (if cooked with oil) or even for weeks (if baked without oil). That said, they may get a bit stale within a week. If so, you can try heating them back up for some additional crisp.

cont'd

SOFT "TOTOPOS"

I first had this spin on totopos while working with Steve Santana at Taquiza restaurant in Miami. Instead of frying a cooked tortilla, Taquiza took an uncooked table tortilla made of blue cónico corn, ripped it into pieces, and dropped them straight into the fryer. The result was an impossibly soft, yet crusty chip that tasted somewhere between a toasted fresh pita and warm Frito, served with guacamole on the side.

INSTRUCTIONS

Heat 4 in [10 cm] of oil to 350°F [180°C] and line a baking sheet with paper towels (optional).

Roll a ping-pong-size ball (about 1½ in [4 cm]) of Table Tortilla Masa (page 114) and press into a thick tortilla (about ⅛ in [3 mm] thick). Carefully remove the plastic liner. Tear the tortilla into quarters, fifths or sixths—rustic, imperfect shapes are fine.

Test a totopo by dropping it into the fryer; if the oil is hot enough, it should sizzle immediately. When ready, drop the pieces of tortilla into the fryer and move them around somewhat continuously until color develops on both sides, 30 to 60 seconds. The totopos should bubble a bit, given the high moisture and fine grind of the table tortilla masa. With a slotted spoon or spider, remove from the fryer and transfer to the paper towels to let excess oil drain (optional). While still hot, quickly transfer to a mixing bowl. Season with fine sea salt, toss, and serve at once.

ASIENTO

Originally hailing from San Bartolomé Quialana, Oaxaca, our friend, chef Juan Hernandez of the Gjelina restaurant group, shared his personal recipe for asiento, which he enjoys most on the large-format huaraches (page 177) of his hometown. Asiento is an optional but common topping or cooking fat used for several of the shapes covered in this section. His version includes bits of pork in it (which I love), however, you can strain the pork meat and use separately for another dish if you prefer.

YIELDS 2½ CUPS (19.45 oz [750 g])

1½ lb [680 g] pork fat back, cut into 1 in [2.5 cm] cubes

1 lb [455 g] pork shoulder, cut into 1 in [2.5 cm] cubes

1 whole head of garlic, peeled

1 tsp salt

Using a heavy-bottom pan over low heat, add the pork fat back and cover with a lid. Cook over low heat for about 30 minutes, allowing the backfat to begin to cook down (render), stirring occasionally. Then add the pork shoulder, garlic, and salt and continue cooking on low heat, stirring often, for about 30 to 40 minutes, or until the pork has browned. Discard the garlic, then strain the fat with a fine-mesh sieve and transfer it to a small bowl. Allow the fat to cool in the fridge while you put the cooked pork in a food processor or blender, and blend the cooked meat for about 1 to 2 minutes, or until you have a nice, grainy paste. Remove the backfat from the fridge and check the consistency; it should be cooled enough to no longer be liquid and should start to turn opaque. If it is still clear and liquid, return to the fridge until it has thickened further. Then fold the pork paste into the cooled fat and mix until well incorporated. Place in an airtight container and continue to stir occasionally as it continues to cool in the fridge (this helps keep the meat suspended in the fat, rather than settled at the bottom). The asiento can be kept refrigerated for a month or in the freezer for up to 3 months.

Topping and Stuffing Basics

With most traditional masa shapes outlined here, you can expect a fairly consistent formula for toppings and/or stuffings to begin your dish assembly. Throughout Mexico and Central America, for example, the holy trinity of cheese, salsa, and beans is a core anchor to a majority of the shapes featured in this section. But, just because these are the most common elements does not mean that they are the *only* ones that you may personally choose from.

Condiments may be my all-time favorite food group, and, as far as I'm concerned, there is no better vessel than masa for exploring their diversity across our global larder. Personally, I love using masa shapes to bring all sorts of leftovers (like roasted chicken, steak, and soups) and/or straight condiments (harissa, chili crisp, onion dip) to life. Here are a few ideas to help get you started.

FATS	CHEESE	SALSAS	BEANS
Asiento, guacamole, schmaltz, coconut oil, butter, olive oil, mayonnaise, sour cream, crème fraîche, yogurt, etc.	Queso fresco, quesillo, cream cheese, Cheddar, ricotta, Gruyère, Ocosingo, "queso," Cotija, feta, etc.	Green, red, habanero, pico de gallo, salsa macha, vinegar-based hot sauce, etc.	Black, pinto, ayocote, fava, etc. (refried, loose purée, whole)

VEGETABLES	HERBS	PROTEIN	ADDITIONAL CONDIMENTS
Shredded lettuce, shredded cabbage, avocado, tomato, chopped onions, jalapeño, pickled vegetables, fermented vegetables, roasted vegetables, etc.	Cilantro, parsley, tarragon, chepiche, mint, basil, etc.	Stewed meat (guisados), roasted meat, picadillo, ceviche, canned fish (sardines, mussels, etc.), caviar, smoked fish, chorizo, eggs, sausage, tofu, plant-based "meats"	Flaked salt, harissa, dips (green goddess, onion, hummus, baba ganoush), Calabrian chili paste, soy sauce, fish sauce, yuzu kosho, Sriracha, chili crisp, gochujang, teriyaki sauce, hoisin, ketchup, mustard, etc.

Modern Masa Explorations

Masa—like coffee or wine, leavened bread or steamed rice—is a culinary force to be reckoned with. And like these staples, while masa's origins can be historically traced to a specific region and culture(s) in the world, there's no denying that it has become something far larger than the place or people from which it originates.

Today, whether at the hands of industry titans like Gruma, third-generation tortillerias like El Milagro, high-end chefs, or home cooks and bloggers, masa is more widely distributed and accessible than at any other point in history. It has transcended time and space to become a formidable fixture of our global pantry, and this trend doesn't seem to be letting up any time soon.

This means that both masa and the dishes that it makes up are in a constant state of evolution. More accurately, it's been evolving since human's first interactions with the stuff; and this metamorphosis is occurring both in contexts that have seemingly little in common with Mesoamerica (a Kenyan taqueria, for instance, or a German tortilleria) as well as in cultures that have directly shaped masa since its beginnings (such as those indigenous communities that continue to thrive throughout the masa foodway).

At no point in the human story has food or culture been static; so too is the case for masa. And to limit this staple to an ephemeral notion of "tradition" would be to miss the point.

The following recipes are a testament to this real-time unfolding of the masa canon. The results may not be "traditional" in the strict sense of the word, but they do begin to demonstrate how much masa has become a shared human experience across cultures. And with any luck, they'll continue to inspire new ways of relating to this timeless, dynamic food.

Chef Carlos Salgado trained in Michelin-starred restaurants in the San Francisco Bay Area before earning his own star for his Alta California–inspired restaurant, Taco María, in Costa Mesa, California. Having worked mostly in pastry prior to opening Taco María, it's somewhat surprising to learn that Carlos rarely serves dessert at his restaurant. If you visit often enough, however, you may be lucky enough to try something he's working on for fun, like the breakfasty coffee atole featured here, or his sublime strawberry tamal (you'll have to ask him for that one).

Coffee Atole

MAKES SIXTEEN 4 OZ [115 G] SERVINGS

4 cups [960 ml] whole milk, plus more as needed

2 cups [480 ml] heavy cream

2¼ cups [200 g] dark-roast coffee beans

1 vanilla bean (preferably Mexican)

6 oz [170 g] Table Tortilla Masa (preferably white, page 114)

7 oz [200 g] evaporated cane sugar

½ tsp kosher salt

Note: Evaporated cane sugar is sold as azúcar morena at Mexican grocers. The two days of steeping develops a deeper flavor, so don't skip that part!

Combine the milk and cream in a large saucepan and bring to a boil, being careful to not let it boil over. While the mixture warms, prepare an ice bath in a large bowl. In a separate medium bowl, place the coffee beans. Split open the vanilla bean and scrape the contents into the bowl. Add the husk and any seeds.

Pour the boiling milk mixture over the beans and vanilla. Set the bowl in the ice bath to cool. Refrigerate for 48 hours, stirring well once after 24 hours.

Strain the mixture through a fine chinois or sieve. Weigh the strained mixture and add more milk to make about 48 oz [1.5 L] (about 6½ cups).

Reserve 12 oz [360 ml] of the infused dairy mixture. Pour the remainder into a large flat-bottomed pot. Warm to 185°F [85°C], until the mixture just simmers around the edges.

Add the reserved dairy mixture to a blender along with the masa and purée until smooth. Strain.

Whisk the strained purée into the pot with the simmering mixture. Turn up the heat slightly and continue stirring carefully until the mixture boils, scraping the bottom with a spatula to avoid scorching.

When the mixture has come to a boil, is uniformly thickened, and no longer has the flavor of raw masa—3 to 5 minutes—remove it from the heat. Whisk in the sugar and salt until dissolved, then strain into another pot or insulated container before serving. Serve immediately. It can be kept hot in a tightly covered container to prevent a skin from forming over the top. If it does form, whisk or shear the atole with an immersion blender just before serving.

Philippine-born chef turned cottage baker Karlo Evaristo first caught our attention at Masienda with his stunning polenta loaves made with blue cónico corn. After first exploring baking in 2019, he went on to launch 61 Hundred Bread, a humble home bakery whose name pays homage to the zip code of his Philippine hometown. Karlo's also a professional photographer—his deft crumb shots are served up nearly daily on his Instagram account, which invariably leads 61 Hundred to sell out within minutes of each post. Following his first experiments with polenta, he had a hunch that masa would make for far more flavorful results. Given what we know about nixtamalization (see page 84) and having tasted the difference for ourselves, we can confidently say that Karlo really nailed this one.

Blue Masa Sourdough Bread

MAKES TWO 1¾ LB [800 G] LOAVES

LEVAIN

1½ oz [45 g] mature sourdough starter

1½ oz [45 ml] warm water (80°F [25°C])

1½ oz [45 g] bread flour

BLUE CORN MASA

1 cup [150 g] blue masa harina

¾ tsp salt

1 cup [240 ml] warm water (80°F [25°C])

2¼ tsp butterfly pea flower (optional, for additional natural color)

or

2½ cups [365 g] fresh Table Tortilla Masa (page 114)

¾ tsp salt

2¼ tsp butterfly pea flower (optional, for additional natural color)

DOUGH

2 cups [450 ml] water

5¼ cups [660 g] bread flour

½ cup [135 g] levain

1 Tbsp [16 g] salt

To make the levain: Combine the mature sourdough starter and water in a mixing bowl. Add the flour and mix well until every bit of flour is hydrated. Transfer to a glass jar or bowl and mark the level before rising, using a rubber band or a marker. Let rise in a warm place (80°F [25°C]) for 2 to 2½ hours until risen by 150 percent.

While the levain is rising, make the masa: Put the masa harina and salt in a bowl and slowly pour in the warm water. Mix until the masa is evenly hydrated. Place in a wide, flat container, cover with a layer of plastic wrap, press down to flatten the masa, and let cool to room temperature.

cont'd

Note: If you were not among those dabbling in sourdough in 2020 and are unsure of where to find mature sourdough starter (see page 250, Resources), you can either create your own (for what it's worth, I, urban homesteader that I am, did not) or purchase some online, at your nearest farmers' market, or, in some cases, at your local bakery (thanks, Lodge Bread!). This recipe calls for Masienda's chef-grade blue masa harina; however, any masa harina will do. The color of the masa had more to do with Karlo's flavor preference than its aesthetic contribution (the masa color in this application does not translate as well), which is why he'll use butterfly pea flower to brighten the loaf. You may also substitute the masa harina and its water ratio for fresh Table Tortilla Masa (page 114), with no additional water required.

Alternatively: Bring the water to a boil, pour it over the butterfly pea flowers, and let it steep (this can be done a few hours in advance). Strain out the flowers, squeezing them to collect as much water as you can. Not all of the water will be squeezed out, so just add a little bit more water to the bowl to bring the measurement back to 1 cup [240 ml]. Warm it up a bit and use this tea to rehydrate the masa in place of the specified 1 cup [240 ml] of water.

An hour before the levain is ready, make the dough: Put the water in the bowl of a stand mixer fitted with a dough hook, then add the bread flour. Mix on low speed until all of the flour is evenly hydrated, 2 to 3 minutes. You do not need to develop gluten at this point (you are using the autolyse method). Cover the bowl and let it sit until the levain is ready. The hydrated dough will develop gluten over time. This is important to give your dough a head start on developing strength and elasticity.

Once the levain has grown in volume by 150 percent, it is ready to be mixed into the dough. You should see bubbles begin to break the surface, and it will smell fruity with a hint of sourness. If you smell alcohol, there's a chance that the levain is overfermented. You may still be able to use it; however, the acid load will compromise the dough structure a bit, and you may prefer redoing the levain.

Once the levain is ready, add it to the mixer together with the salt and mix until well dispersed. If you do this by hand, make sure to really mix well, until all of the salt is dissolved and the levain is well incorporated. Cover the bowl and let it sit for 30 minutes.

After 30 minutes, stretch and fold the dough. With wet hands, dig your hand into the 12 o'clock position of the dough, grabbing the underside of the dough, and stretch it toward you as much as you can without the dough tearing. Repeat this around the entire circumference of the dough. Cover and let sit for another 30 minutes.

After 30 minutes, put the masa mixture on top of the dough. You will now stretch and fold again, but this time you'll stretch the dough over the masa and cover it entirely. After this, attach the bowl to the mixer with a hook attachment and mix on low until the masa is completely incorporated.

Grease a bowl with a neutral oil, such as grapeseed, or a pan spray. Using a dough spatula, transfer the dough into the bowl. The dough will be very wet and sticky; this is normal. Let it sit for 15 minutes.

After 15 minutes, stretch and fold the dough. Let rest, and repeat twice more at 15-minute intervals. By this time, the dough should have developed enough strength that it will start to hold its shape better. The goal is to stop folding once the dough holds a slight dome surface.

Let the dough rest until the volume increases about 50 percent, about 4 hours. The fermentation will cause bubbles to form in the surface and around the sides of the bowl.

To test, cut a piece of the dough and place it a bowl of water. If it floats, it is ready. If it sinks to the bottom, it is not ready.

Turn the dough out onto an unfloured surface and divide it into two equal pieces.

With a bench knife, shape the dough into a rounded ball by positioning the bench knife at 2 o'clock and scraping under the dough to lift it toward 7 o'clock while your left hand supports the dough (if you're left-handed, lift from 11 o'clock to 5 o'clock). This stretches the surface tension of the dough so you end up with a nice, tight, smooth ball of dough. Repeat with the other piece of dough.

cont'd

Cover with a lightly damp towel and let it sit for 45 minutes. The dough should start to flatten out but still maintain its rounded edges.

Once the dough has relaxed, it's time to add strength one final time. Sprinkle a little bit of flour on top of the dough. With a bench knife, scoop up the dough and place it floured-side down on a floured surface.

Lift the entire bottom and fold two-thirds of it over. Then stretch both sides of the folded dough and pull them into the center, overlapping each other. Grab the top flap and fold into the middle. Now, using the thumb and index finger of each hand, starting from the top left and right corners, "zip" or "stitch" the dough down the middle by pulling the outer edge inward, all the way to the bottom.

At this point, you can grab the very top flap with your fingers and lift and fold it to meet the bottom flap. Place this, seam-side up, in a banneton or large mixing bowl dusted with rice flour.

Cover the dough with a lightly damp towel and refrigerate for 12 to 18 hours. Refrigerating the dough slows down the fermentation process but also develops the flavor of the loaf even further. Just make sure the dough has proofed enough at room temperature first, because chilling will drastically slow the fermentation.

When ready to bake, center a rack in the oven and preheat a cast iron pot or Dutch oven with a lid at 500°F [260°C] for at least one hour.

Carefully remove the pot from the oven and remove the lid. Take the dough from the refrigerator and carefully drop it into the pot, seam-side down.

With a paring knife, slice or score the top of the loaf. This will help the loaf expand in the oven. Place the lid on the pot and bake for 20 minutes.

After 20 minutes, carefully remove the lid and lower the oven temperature to 450°F [230°C]. Bake for another 20 minutes or until the crust is nice and brown.

To test for doneness, tap the bottom of the loaf. When done, the loaf should sound hollow.

Cool for at least 1 to 2 hours before serving.

This masa tempura batter is the key to Empellón's fried fish taco, one of the restaurant's most popular dishes. The batter can be used on just about any host, from fish and shrimp to vegetables and tofu. Alex's secret to getting an even, flaky consistency from this masa batter is to run it through a cream whipper. Cream whippers work by using compressed nitrous oxide to aerate the liquid inside through a nozzle at the top. If you don't have one of these lying around, you can get pretty close by whisking or blending the batter for a bit longer, as you might to whip cream, for 2 to 3 minutes, until smooth and even.

Masa Tempura Batter

MAKES 4 SERVINGS (2¼ CUPS [540 ML] TEMPURA BATTER)

1 to 2 qt [1 to 2 L] vegetable oil, for frying

2 cups [475 ml] cold water

1 cup [125 g] masa harina, plus more for dredging

½ tsp fine salt, plus more for seasoning

1 lb [455 g] shrimp, fish, or tofu, or 4 cups [about 480 g] thinly sliced vegetables

Freshly ground black pepper

Fill a deep fryer or pot with at least 2 in [5 cm] of oil and heat to 350°F [180°C].

In a blender, combine the water, masa harina, and salt and blend on high speed until smooth. (If you're not using a cream whipper, blend for 2 to 3 minutes more.) Strain the batter through a fine-mesh sieve into a bowl and refrigerate until cold. If using a cream whipper, pour the batter into the cream whipper and express the batter through the nozzle into a bowl.

Season the shrimp or other tempura-dipping ingredients with salt and pepper. Pour extra masa harina for dredging into a bowl. Dredge the shrimp in the masa harina, shaking off the excess. Next, dip the shrimp into the chilled batter until fully coated and then carefully lower into the hot oil, making sure not to overcrowd them in the pot. Fry in batches, flipping halfway through, until golden brown, 3 to 5 minutes. Strain on a wire rack or paper towel–lined plate, season with more salt, and serve hot.

This dish hails from the short-lived but highly impressive Lalo restaurant in New York City. Chef-owner Gerardo Gonzalez, who previously ran the perennially popular El Rey in NYC's Lower East Side, brought Chicano cooking to the fore, with flourishes of Middle Eastern, Japanese, Chinese, and even Ashkenazi-Jewish traditions. In addition to his eclectic set of atoles (one was memorably made with the locally contraband Tonka bean), he used masa to make the most hauntingly delicious version of gnocchi that I've ever had. Finished in a lamb birria, this dish is a two- to three-day project, but it is well worth the wait! I'd recommend brining the lamb shanks on the first day, making the gnocchi dough and braising the lamb on the second day, and cooking the gnocchi on the third day for best results.

Lamb Birria with Masa Gnocchi

MAKES 6 SERVINGS
(can be scaled up or down)

LAMB BIRRIA

4 lb [1.8 kg] lamb shank (see Note)

4 lb [1.8 kg] lamb neck (see Note)

1½ cups [360 ml] distilled white vinegar

½ cup [80 g] Diamond Crystal kosher salt or ¼ cup [60 g] fine salt or Morton's kosher salt, plus more for seasoning

15 bay leaves

½ cup [50 g] cumin seeds, toasted

¼ cup [50 g] whole black peppercorns

2 Tbsp coriander seeds

1 cinnamon stick

10 guajillo peppers, seeded

2 ancho chiles, seeded

1 white onion, peeled and halved

6 garlic cloves, peeled

5 cups [1.2 L] vegetable or chicken stock

1 large tomato, cut into large chunks

Freshly ground black pepper

MASA GNOCCHI

1½ cups [185 g] masa harina

1 Tbsp vegetable or chicken flavor bouillon powder (such as Maggi or Knorr brands)

¾ tsp ground cumin

¾ tsp baking powder

½ tsp Diamond Crystal kosher salt or ¼ tsp fine salt or Morton's kosher salt, plus more for seasoning

3½ cups [830 ml] cold water

1⅓ cups [315 ml] vegetable broth, warmed

½ cup [120 g] pork lard or vegetable shortening

Hojas de tamales, rehydrated, or banana leaves, for steaming

FOR SERVING

Finely diced white onion

Chopped fresh oregano

Thinly sliced radish

Chopped fresh cilantro

Lime wedges

Note: The lamb in this recipe can easily be swapped for goat or beef. If you can't find a neck cut, you can replace it with more shank, shoulder, or other stew-meat cuts.

To start the lamb birria: Rinse the meat and place in a 6 qt [5.7 L] or larger pot or container.

In a small saucepan over low heat, whisk together the vinegar, salt, and cold water until dissolved. Cool and pour over the meat. Cover and refrigerate for 24 hours.

The next day, in a medium pot, combine the bay leaves, cumin, peppercorns, coriander, cinnamon, chiles, half of the onion, and the garlic. Add just enough water to cover and enough salt so that it tastes salty like the ocean. Bring to a boil over high heat, then decrease to a simmer and cook until a fork can easily be inserted and removed from the onion and garlic, about 35 minutes. Using a slotted spoon, transfer the cooked onion, garlic, chiles, and all of the spices, except for the cinnamon stick, to a blender. Blend on high speed to make a paste, adding some of the cooking liquid as needed to loosen, and blend well. Set aside.

To start the masa gnocchi: In a large bowl, whisk together the masa harina, bouillon powder, cumin, baking powder, and salt. Using a wooden spoon, stir the warm vegetable broth into the masa mixture to form a thick dough.

In a separate bowl, whip the lard with an electric mixer fitted with a paddle attachment until fluffy, about 1 minute. Add one-third of the masa mixture to the lard and gently mix until fully incorporated. Continue adding the masa mixture, one-third at a time, until smooth. Mix in enough warm water to loosen the dough to the consistency of a thick cake batter or smooth mashed potatoes, about ½ cup plus 2 Tbsp [150 ml]. Cover the masa mixture with plastic wrap and refrigerate for 12 to 24 hours.

To finish the lamb birria: Remove the lamb from the brine and place into a 6 qt [5.7 L] or larger Dutch oven. Slather the lamb with the chile paste. Add the stock, remaining half of the onion (cut into quarters, if needed), and tomato, and bring to a boil over high heat. Decrease the heat to a low simmer, cover the pot, and braise on the stovetop until the meat easily falls off the bone, about 2 hours.

cont'd

Remove the meat from the broth. Let cool slightly, then pull the meat from the bones. Discard the bones and set the meat aside. Strain the remaining broth into a large sauté pan, pressing on the solids to extract their juices. The liquid should be brothy, with a little body and fat emulsified in. Simmer over medium-low heat until the broth is reduced by one-third. Add the pulled lamb pieces to the broth and bring to a low simmer. Season to taste with salt and pepper. Set aside and let cool, then place in the refrigerator and let the braised lamb sit overnight in the finished broth to let the flavors meld.

To cook the masa gnocchi: The next day, put the rested masa dough in a 1 qt [1 L] plastic or piping bag with no tip. Cut the tip of the bag 1 in [2.5 cm].

Using a double bain steamer: Place a double bain steamer on the stovetop. Line the steamer with hydrated hojas de tamales or banana leaves. Add enough water to the bottom of the steamer to rise 1 in [2.5 cm] high, then add just enough salt to the water so that it tastes salty like the ocean. Pipe the masa onto the hojas de tamales into 6 to 8 in [15 to 20 cm] logs, spacing them 1 in [2.5 cm] apart. Place a cover on the steamer, decrease the heat to a simmer, and steam the logs for 15 to 20 minutes.

Using a rimmed baking sheet: If you do not have a double bain steamer, you can create a makeshift steamer by placing a cooling rack on a rimmed baking sheet. Preheat the oven to 425°F [220°C]. Add enough water to the baking sheet to rise 1 in [2.5 cm] high, then add just enough salt to the water so that it tastes salty like the ocean. Line the cooling rack with the hydrated hojas de tamales or banana leaves and place over the baking sheet. Pipe the masa onto the hojas de tamales into 6 to 8 in [15 to 20 cm] logs, spacing them 1 in [2.5 cm] apart. Cover the baking sheet with tented foil and bake for 15 to 20 minutes.

Remove from the heat, uncover, and let rest. Once done, the dough will be slightly soft and malleable but will set as it rests. Repeat, as needed, with the remaining dough.

Cut the masa logs into 1 in [2.5 cm] gnocchi dumplings. Add the gnocchi to the lamb broth and simmer for 5 to 8 minutes until fully set yet fluffy and very soft.

To serve: Ladle the gnocchi and lamb with some sauce into shallow bowls. Garnish with diced onion, oregano, radish, and cilantro, and finish with a squeeze of fresh lime juice.

Chef Daniela Soto-Innes exploded onto the global culinary scene as chef de cuisine of New York City's Cosme and Atla restaurants, where she led both kitchens until 2020. Daniela's cooking and personality are full of energy, and watching her at work, it can literally be exercise to try to keep up with her, let alone replicate what she's doing. Given that some of her more noteworthy dishes have already been well documented, such as Cosme's duck carnitas and iconic corn husk merengue, I asked Daniela to share her favorite pro tip for using masa at work or at home—and to be sure it was something that a cook of any experience level could easily follow!

Since my earliest days researching masa, I'd always known that it could be used as an emulsifier, thickener, or hydrocolloid of sorts, but I never fully appreciated just how dynamic its application range could really be. As a former line cook, I was accustomed to using xanthan gum for certain finishing sauces, but for Daniela and her team, masa is the standard. Whipped or blended with water into a light slurry, she uses it in everything from moles and stews to mayonnaise and salad dressing.

In her take on chilpachole, a traditional seafood stew from Veracruz, for example, Daniela uses this masa slurry to achieve a silky, creamy texture, much like a bisque, but without the dairy. For a vegetarian approach, you can replace the crab and stock with vegetables like broccoli and a simple vegetable broth. And, if soft shells aren't in season, substitute them with shell-on shrimp for both the stock and dish itself.

Chilpachole

MAKES 4 SERVINGS

CRAB STOCK

1 lb [455 g] crab shells

1 Tbsp olive oil

¼ white onion, chopped

½ carrot, chopped

1 celery stalk, chopped

2 bay leaves

1½ tsp black peppercorns

2 qt [2 L] water

To make the crab stock: In a large pot, combine the crab shells, olive oil, onion, carrot, celery, bay leaves, peppercorns, and water. Bring to a boil over high heat, then decrease the heat to medium-low and simmer for 30 minutes. Strain through a fine-mesh sieve. Set aside 2 cups [475 ml]. (Refrigerate or freeze the remainder for use in other seafood recipes.)

To make the chilpachole: In a large saucepan over medium heat, heat the grapeseed oil. Add the onion, garlic, chiles, and epazote and sauté, stirring often, for about 1 minute. Add the crabs and cook, flipping them often, until bright orange all over, about 5 minutes. Transfer the crabs to a cutting board, cut them in half lengthwise, and keep warm under tented foil. Add the tomatoes to the saucepan and

CHILPACHOLE

2 Tbsp grapeseed oil

¼ white onion, roughly chopped

2 garlic cloves, roughly chopped

8 guajillo chiles, stemmed and seeded

1 pasilla chile, stemmed and seeded

6 sprigs fresh epazote

2 soft-shell crabs (3 to 4 oz [85 to 115 g] each)

6 plum tomatoes, cut into chunks

2 cups [475 ml] Crab Stock (recipe precedes)

1¾ oz [50 g] Table Tortilla Masa (page 114), made with white corn

Salt

2 Tbsp cold-pressed, extra-virgin olive oil

simmer, covered, stirring occasionally to release their juices, about 15 minutes.

In a small saucepan, bring the 2 cups [480 ml] of strained crab stock to a simmer. Lower in the table tortilla masa dough piece by piece and whisk until nearly smooth. Add this slurry mixture to the tomato-chile mixture and simmer over medium-low heat, uncovered, for 20 minutes longer. Season with salt.

Transfer the contents of the saucepan to a blender and purée on high speed until smooth. Strain through a fine-mesh sieve back into the saucepan. Reheat if needed and season as needed with salt. Ladle the soup into four bowls, top each with a soft-shell crab half, and drizzle with ½ Tbsp of cold-pressed olive oil. Serve hot.

MASA AS A THICKENER

Masa is used in moles and stews, like cuachala (from Jalisco and Colima, Mexico), as a thickening agent. In this sense, it may be thought of as a hydrocolloid, or simple emulsifying agent. The incorporation of masa into a soup will give it a porridge-like consistency, while a mole will develop a tighter body as a result.

If I could choose one word to describe Sean Brock's approach to cooking, it would be *reverence*. In addition to his remarkable talent in the kitchen, I have especially always admired his soft-spoken, humble approach to the study of American cuisine and how he thoughtfully, artfully, and graciously celebrates its connection to diverse cultures across the world. While his upbringing in rural Virginia and life study of Southern foodways might seem at odds with the Mesoamerican tradition of masa, they are, in fact, what makes his approach to masa so personal and compelling. It was, after all, an upbringing of preparing hominy (see pozole, page 145) with his grandmother Audrey—namesake of his flagship restaurant in Nashville, Tennessee—that got him into nixtamal from an early age.

In this twist on a Southern favorite, grits are swapped out for smooth, cooked masa that's been flavored with milk. You'll have plenty of leftover sofrito; use it to flavor chicken or beans, or just slather it on a tostada (page 213). If you don't see yourself using it immediately, it freezes well, too. True to tradition, Sean is especially fond of nixtamal prepared with wood ash (see page 88), but cal will perform just as well.

Shrimp and (Masa) Grits

MAKES 4 SERVINGS

SOFRITO

1 medium yellow onion, quartered

1 large or two small carrot(s), scrubbed

2 large tomatoes

8 to 10 small tomatillos (about 5 oz [140 g]), husked and rinsed

1 medium poblano pepper

1 small red bell pepper

2 garlic cloves, unpeeled

1 pasilla chile

1 tablespoon aji amarillo powder or 1 whole aji amarillo

GRITS

3 cups [720 ml] whole milk

12 oz [340 g] Table Tortilla Masa (page 114)

cont'd

To make the sofrito: Heat a comal or cast-iron skillet or grill over medium-low heat. Working in batches so as to not overcrowd the pan, cook the onion, carrots, tomatoes, tomatillos, poblano, bell pepper, and garlic, turning every so often until they're deeply charred in spots all over. For the peppers, the skin should be evenly charred and the flesh soft. Wrap the peppers in a kitchen towel for 15 to 20 minutes to steam, then peel and remove the seeds. Place the garlic at the edge of the comal—away from direct heat—and toast until browned in spots and soft. Remove the charred garlic skins and discard.

Toast the pasilla chile and whole aji amarillo, if using. Steam and remove the seeds, then rehydrate by submerging the chile in hot water for about 15 minutes. Meanwhile, roughly chop the larger charred vegetables. Drain the chiles and discard the soaking water. Put the vegetables and chiles in a food processor and blend until smooth.

cont'd

2 Tbsp unsalted butter, diced, at room temperature

Salt

SHRIMP

20 large shrimp, peeled and deveined

1 Tbsp canola oil

Salt

1 chorizo, cooked and crumbled

GARNISH

1 cup [48 g] thinly sliced scallions, white and green parts

1 cup [120 g] crumbled Cotija cheese

1 cup [12 g] packed cilantro leaves

4 lime wedges

Hot sauce (such as Valentina)

Cook the mixture in a nonreactive pot over medium heat, stirring constantly, until the mixture has darkened slightly and reduced by half, about 30 minutes. Cover the sofrito and keep warm.

To make the grits: In a medium saucepan, bring the milk to a simmer over high heat. Crumble the masa into the milk and turn the heat to low. Cook, stirring constantly, for 20 minutes. The mixture may be a little lumpy at first, but don't worry, the lumps break down as the mixture cooks. Add the butter and season with salt. Cover and keep warm.

To make the shrimp: Toss the shrimp in the canola oil and season with salt. If using a grill, grill for 3 to 5 minutes. Alternatively, heat a large frying pan over medium-high heat and cook the shrimp in one layer (in batches if necessary) until opaque, about 1 minute per side. Remove from the heat.

In a medium bowl, toss the shrimp with the cooked chorizo and 1 cup [120 g] of the sofrito.

To serve, place ½ cup [70 g] of grits in each bowl. Top with shrimp and garnish with a heavy toss of scallion, cheese, and cilantro. Serve with lime wedges and hot sauce.

When you meet chef Saw Naing, it's hard not be charmed by his earnest, genuine passion for masa. His deep love for this staple is a case study in how geographically disparate cultures can find common ground, respect, and even deep admiration for one another through food. After immigrating from Burma at the age of twenty-one, Saw fell into cooking as a means of paying his way through music school. He ultimately ended up pursuing food full time, working for chefs Thomas Keller and Jeremy Fox, before becoming executive chef of Tallula's, a casual Mexican restaurant in Santa Monica, California. Lacking the money or visa to experience Mexico firsthand, he learned about its cuisine in any way he could—through books, local restaurants, industry friends, and, most important, his fellow Mexican cooks. Saw describes Mexican and Burmese cooking as culinary soul siblings; as he gained confidence, he began blending references, techniques, and flavor profiles of his Burmese roots into the menu at Tallula's. Originally served as a Puffy Taco (page 187), Saw's masa samosa is his grandmother's samosa filling applied to a crispy empanada (page 167).

Masa Samosas

MAKES 25 TO 40 SAMOSAS

POTATO FILLING

2 lb [910 g] Yukon gold potatoes (about 7 medium), skin on

½ cup [80 g] Diamond Crystal kosher salt or ¼ cup [60 g] fine salt or Morton's kosher salt, plus more as needed

1 cup [240 ml] olive oil

2 garlic cloves, peeled and smashed

1 Tbsp cumin seeds

1 Tbsp black mustard seeds

2 Tbsp garam masala

1 large white onion, cut into ⅓ in [8.5 mm] slices

1 cup [40 g] roughly chopped cilantro (about 1 large bunch)

Freshly ground black pepper

cont'd

To make the potato filling: Put the potatoes in a large pasta pot with 4 qt [3.8 L] of cold water and the salt and bring to a boil. Once boiling, lower the heat and simmer for 20 minutes, or until the potatoes can be easily pierced with a fork. Using a slotted spoon, scoop the potatoes from the water and let cool.

While the potatoes are simmering, in a large sauté pan or skillet, heat the olive oil over medium-low heat. Add the garlic, cumin seeds, and mustard seeds and cook until simmering, about 4 minutes. Add the garam masala and cook for about 3 minutes longer. Remove the garlic cloves and discard. Add the onion and cook over medium-low heat until softened, about 30 minutes. Season to taste with salt.

Once the potatoes have cooled, place in a medium bowl and roughly smash them, peel-on, with a fork or potato masher.

cont'd

Puffy Taco (page 187) or
Empanada (page 167)

About 1 qt [945 ml] canola oil,
for frying

Stir the potatoes into the cooked onion mixture. Fold in the chopped cilantro and generously season with salt and pepper.

To make the samosas: Using the puffy taco or empanada as a base, add 2 to 3 Tbsp of filling per samosa and fold into triangles.

Fill a saucepan with 2 in [5 cm] of oil. Heat the oil over medium-high heat to 350°F [180°C]. Carefully lower the samosas into the hot oil, without crowding. Fry in batches until golden brown, 1 to 3 minutes per side. Transfer to a wire rack or paper towel–lined plate. Repeat with the remaining samosas, replenishing and reheating the oil between batches as needed.

Having trained under molecular gastronomy legends Grant Achatz and Wylie Dufresne, Alex Stupak was a young pastry prodigy before applying his talents to masa at Empellón in New York City. Alex has a deep devotion to Mexican cuisine, but he's not afraid to mash up traditional techniques with modern flavors, as in these Masa Corn Dogs.

Huitlacoche, also known as cuitlacoche, corn truffle, or corn smut, is best when fresh.

Because fresh huitlacoche only lasts about 7 to 10 days refrigerated, it can be difficult to find. It will usually be located in the refrigerated area of the produce section of your local Latin grocer.

If you are unable to find fresh huitlacoche, canned huitlacoche may be substituted here. Just make sure to strain out all of the canning liquid before use. Canned huitlacoche is available online and at most Latin grocers.

Masa Corn Dog (with Huitlacoche "Mustard")

MAKES 8 SERVINGS

HUITLACOCHE MUSTARD

1 Tbsp olive oil

3 Tbsp finely chopped onion

2 large garlic cloves, finely chopped

1 small serrano chile, seeded, deveined, and finely chopped

1 medium tomato, roughly chopped

7 oz [200 g] fresh huitlacoche or one 7 oz [198 g] can huitlacoche (corn smut), rinsed and drained

⅓ cup plus 1 Tbsp [100 g] Dijon mustard

2 tsp mezcal

½ tsp sugar

½ tsp MSG

¼ tsp fish sauce

cont'd

To make the huitlacoche mustard: Heat the olive oil in a medium sauté pan over medium-low heat. Add the onion, garlic, and chile and cook until softened, 3 to 5 minutes. Add the tomato and cook, stirring and raising the heat to medium as needed, to release and then evaporate the juices, about 5 minutes. Add the huitlacoche and cook until its juices have released and evaporated, 3 to 5 minutes more. Transfer to a blender. Add the Dijon mustard, mezcal, sugar, MSG, and fish sauce, and purée on high speed until smooth. Transfer to a bowl and set aside.

To make the corn dogs: Crumble the masa into a blender. Add the milk, egg, and salt, and purée on high speed until combined. Transfer to a large bowl. Fold in the flour, baking powder, and calcium hydroxide until just combined. (The mixture will thicken a bit as it sits.) Let rest for 5 minutes and use immediately thereafter.

cont'd

CORN DOGS

1 lb [455 g] Table Tortilla Masa
(page 114)

About 1 cup [240 ml] milk

1 large egg

1 tsp fine salt

3 Tbsp all-purpose flour

1 tsp baking powder

1 tsp calcium hydroxide (lime)

2 qt [1.9 L] vegetable oil, for frying

8 hot dogs

Chili salt

Lime wedges, for serving

In a pot that's 2 in [5 cm] wider than the skewers, heat 3 in [7.5 cm] of oil to 350°F [180°C]. Insert a skewer lengthwise through the center of each hot dog, leaving 1 in [2.5 cm] or so of skewer exposed at the end.

Fill a 1 pt [480 ml] glass with the batter. Submerge a hot dog into the batter, coating it all over. Fry one or two hot dogs at a time, depending on the size of your pot, until golden brown, 4 to 5 minutes. Let drain on a wire rack or paper towel–lined plate. Season with chili salt. Repeat until all the hot dogs are fried. Serve the corn dogs with lime wedges and the huitlacoche mustard on the side.

I had never personally experimented much with sweet pastry items of any sort, but I knew it could be done easily with masa. After all, masa appears in not only savory applications throughout Mesoamerica but also plenty of confections, like the rosquilla cookies of Nicaragua and turuletes of southern Mexico (Chiapas and Tabasco).

I asked our friend Jess Stephens, who herself worked at the Modern Mexican pastry programs at the restaurants Empellón and Onda, to develop a few sweet dishes for Masienda, including these Masa Harina Waffles and White Chocolate Chip Cookies (page 250).

Masa Harina Waffle

MAKES 4 WAFFLES

3 egg whites

3 Tbsp sugar

2 cups [480 ml] buttermilk

1 egg yolk

6 Tbsp [85 g] butter, melted

1½ cups [210 g] all-purpose flour

1 cup [140 g] masa harina

2 tsp baking powder

1 tsp baking soda

1 tsp salt

Note (Optional): If you happen to have extra sourdough starter on hand, you can substitute it for up to half of the buttermilk, for waffles with a little pucker.

Whip the egg whites and sugar until medium stiff peaks form. In a separate bowl, whisk the buttermilk, egg yolk, and melted butter until evenly combined. In a separate bowl, combine the flour, masa harina, baking powder, baking soda, and salt. Alternate whisking in ½ cup [120 ml] of water and the buttermilk mixture. Fold in the egg white mixture. Allow the batter to sit at room temperature for at least 10 minutes for the corn to soften. The batter will be thick, as the masa harina will absorb much of the liquid. Follow your waffle maker's instructions for baking, and serve with your favorite toppings.

White Chocolate Chip Cookies

MAKES 2 DOZEN COOKIES

1 cup [180 g] white chocolate chips or chopped bars

2⅓ cups [280 g] all-purpose flour

⅓ cup [50 g] masa harina

½ tsp baking soda

1 tsp salt

1¼ cups [275 g] butter, at room temperature

½ cup [100 g] granulated sugar

¾ cup [150 g] packed light brown sugar

2 eggs

1 tsp vanilla extract

⅔ cup [100 g] chopped macadamia nuts

Flaky salt (optional)

Preheat the oven to 325°F [165°C] and line a rimmed baking sheet with a silicone mat or parchment paper. Spread out the white chocolate on the lined pan. (This is going to get gooey, so do not put the chocolate directly onto a baking sheet, or it will absorb the flavors of every one-sheet-pan dinner that came before.) Bake the chocolate for 5 minutes, or until you see some browning along the edges. Stir the chocolate and repeat until all of the chocolate is the color of light amber honey. This happens slowly at first and then quickly, so keep an eye on the oven. It shouldn't take more than 15 minutes. Allow the caramelized chocolate to cool completely before breaking it up into chunks for the cookies.

Combine the flour, masa harina, baking soda, and salt in a bowl, whisk together, and set aside. In the bowl of a stand mixer, cream the butter, granulated sugar, and light brown sugar for a few minutes, until fluffy and pale. With the mixer running, add the eggs, one at a time, and then the vanilla. Mix until just combined. Add the flour mixture in increments until evenly incorporated. Fold in the chopped macadamias and caramelized white chocolate pieces. Press a plastic sheet onto the top of the dough and refrigerate the bowl for at least 30 minutes before scooping.

Preheat the oven to 375°F [190°C] and grease a baking sheet. Scoop the dough into 2 in [5 cm] clumps and space them evenly on the prepared pan, with at least 4 in [10 cm] of space between them. Top the dough with flaky salt, if you're so inclined. Bake for 6 minutes and rotate the sheet. Bake for another 6 minutes, or until the cookies are slightly brown on the edges and just set in the middle. Cool the cookies for as long as you can stand it and serve.

Resources

AMAZON
pH meters, laser thermometers, atomizers, digital scales, tequesquites
amazon.com

AZTECA MACHINE SHOP
A basalt stone sharpening specialist
626.579.5701

CONABIO
For a full list of landrace corn varieties and information
gob.mx/conabio

ETSY
Sifted wood ash, bread starter, tortilla warmers
etsy.com

FRESH MASA AND TORTILLA PURVEYORS
Visit masienda.com for an up-to-date list of exceptional second- and third-wave masa purveyors near you

MASIENDA
The one-stop shop for single-origin corn, masa harina, cal, tortilla presses, comals, molinos, hand mills, tortilla warmers (tortilleros), and other specialty masa-occasion ingredients, as well as resources, recipes, and other masa educational content. Both retail and wholesale available. Fulfills internationally
masienda.com

WEBSTAURANT STORE
Spiders, hotel pans, spatulas, slotted spoons, fine-mesh skimmers, and additional kitchen supplies
webstaurantstore.com

Appendix

Stone sharpening/picking

While stone sharpening/picking is certainly achievable with practice, the ideal tools (a ¾ in [2 cm] carbide chisel and air compressor system *or* a rotary saw with a diamond blade) and space required (think dust and noise) make it difficult for most to do at home or in a restaurant. For this reason, I recommend that you ship your stones to a basalt stone specialist who will do the job for you. Although the service will run about $75 plus shipping, you stand to get more longevity out of the stones when they're professionally serviced.

Azteca Machine Shop in Los Angeles is the only public business I have come into contact with that truly specializes in this craft, though some restaurants we work with sometimes "have a guy" or an in-house cook, usually from Mexico, who will service their stones for them.

Prior to picking, even if you're sending the stones out to Azteca, you'll want to run wet sand (specifically, silver sand #20, available in 2½ lb [1.2 kg] increments at Masienda or 100 lb [45.4 kg] increments at Home Depot) through your stones to recalibrate the surface and partially erase the stones' working surfaces. This step is critical to ensuring that the stones rest flush against one another and match the unique settings of your molino.

To use, you'll want to moisten the sand to the consistency of wet masa. About 1 cup [240 ml] of water per 2½ lb [1.2 kg] of sand will get you to the right consistency.

Next, with the machine running, run the wet sand through the auger into the stones. The stones should be pressed tightly together as if you were grinding table tortilla masa. Continue to tighten the stones as the sand moves through them. It will smell like burning, but this is normal. You are literally grinding down the face of your stones to a largely fresh face, though the center cavity does not need to be ground down in this preparation.

About 2½ lb [1.2 kg] of sand with the recommended water ratio should do the trick on a 5 in [12 cm] set of stones like those of the Molinito (available at Masienda). The outer half of the lines of the stone face should be erased with this step, leaving the cavity grooves as guides for recarving fresh lines.

Seasoning a carbon steel or cast-iron comal

It's important to know the smoke point of any oil you use to season a comal. Many oils have the smoke point listed on the label. If yours does not, you can refer to this list of common oils. Keep in mind that smoke points can vary depending on the extraction method, source, and so on, so consider these temperatures as approximate guides.

Canola oil: 400°F to 450°F [200°C to 230°C]

Flaxseed oil (unrefined): 250°F to 325°F [120°C to 165°C]

Grapeseed oil: 425°F [220°C]

Peanut oil: 400°F to 450°F [200°C to 230°C]

Sesame oil (unrefined): 350°F [180°C]

Sesame oil (semi-refined): 450°F [232°C]

Sunflower oil: 425°F to 450°F [220°C to 230°C]

Vegetable oil: 425°F [220°C]

pH chart

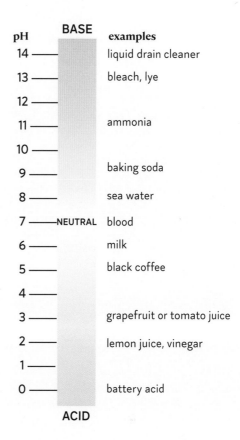

pH		examples
	BASE	
14		liquid drain cleaner
13		bleach, lye
12		
11		ammonia
10		
9		baking soda
8		sea water
7	NEUTRAL	blood
6		milk
5		black coffee
4		
3		grapefruit or tomato juice
2		lemon juice, vinegar
1		
0		battery acid
	ACID	

Bibliography

Adams, Paul. "Transforming Corn: The Science of Nixtamalization." *Cooks Illustrated*, August 14, 2016. www.cooksillustrated.com/science/789-articles/feature/transforming-corn

Arellano, Gustavo. *Taco USA*. New York: Scribner, 2013.

Bayless, Rick, and Deann Groen. *Authentic Mexican*, twentieth anniversary ed. New York: Harper Collins, 1987, 2007.

Coe, Sophie. *America's First Cuisines*. Austin: University of Texas Press, 1994.

Conaculta, Coordinación de Patrimonio, Cultural, Desarrollo y Turismo, July 2005. www.cultura.gob.mx/turismo-cultural/cuadernos/pdf/cuaderno10.pdf.

Fussell, Betty. *The Story of Corn*. Albuquerque, NM: University of New Mexico Press, 2004 (original edition New York: North Point Press, 1992).

Jayasanker, Laresh. *Sameness in Diversity: Food and Globalization in Modern America*. Berkeley: University of California Press, 2020.

Kennedy, Diana. *Oaxaca al Gusto: An Infinite Gastronomy*. Austin: University of Texas Press, 2010.

Kennedy, Diana. *The Art of Mexican Cooking*. New York: Clarkson Potter, 1989, 2008.

Kennedy, Diana. *The Cuisines of Mexico*. New York: Harper and Row, 1972.

McGee, Harold. *On Food and Cooking: The Science and Lore of the Kitchen*. New York: Scribner, 1984, 2004.

Nahuatl Dictionary. nahuatl.uoregon.edu/.

Olvera, Enrique. *Mexico from the Inside Out*. New York: Phaidon Press, 2015.

Pilcher, Jeffrey M. "Industrial Tortillas and Folkloric Pepsi: The Nutritional Consequences of Hybrid Cuisines in Mexico." In *Food Nations: Selling Taste in Consumer Societies,* ed. Warren James Belasco and Philip Scranton, chapter 14. New York: Routledge, 2001.

Pilcher, Jeffrey M. *Que Vivan Los Tamales! Food and the Making of Mexican Identity*. Albuquerque, NM: University of New Mexico Press, 1998.

Rothman, Jordana, and Alex Stupak. *Tacos: Recipes and Provocations*. New York: Clarkson Potter, 2015.

Visser, Margaret. *Much Depends on Dinner*. New York: Harper Collins, 1986.

Zurita, Ricardo Muñoz. *Larousse Diccionario Enciclopédico de la Gastronomía Mexicana*. México, D.F.: Ediciones Larousse, 2012.

Glossary

acid: Having a pH less than 7.0; acidic liquids contain a higher concentration of hydrogen ions than pure water.

alkali: A substance with a pH greater than 7.0 (that is, a base) that is soluble in water.

asiento: Derived from the Spanish verb *asentar* ("to settle"), asiento is the Oaxacan name for a type of lard commonly used for masa dishes throughout the state. It specifically refers to the settled fat that remains after rendering, frying, and cooling pork, most often chicharrón (pork rind).

basalt: A type of rock formed from low-viscosity lava.

base: A substance with a pH greater than 7.0 (that is, alkaline); liquid forms contain a lower concentration of hydrogen ions than pure water.

basic: Of or relating to a base (alkaline).

cal: Spanish term referring to either calcium oxide or calcium hydroxide.

cal viva: Spanish term referring to calcium oxide, usually in rock form; unslaked lime or simply lime.

comal: A flat griddle made of earthenware or metal (plural comals or comales).

endosperm: Broken out into "soft" and "hard" endosperms, this is where the corn's natural protein and starch are derived—both being key emulsifying agents in masa. They are what provide the nutrients to—and protection of—the seed's embryo, or germ.

foodway: Eating habits and cooking practices of a people, region, or historical period.

frying tortilla: A tortilla with a coarse grind and low moisture (around 30 percent) designed for frying.

germ: This is the embryo of the corn and the only living part of the kernel. It is literally a tiny plant inside the seed. All of the kernel's natural oils are derived from the germ, another key emulsifying agent, when ground into masa.

GMO: Genetically modified organism. An organism whose genetic makeup is manipulated to contain genetics that do not naturally occur in the organism itself.

hard endosperm: Also known as the horneous (or "horny") endosperm, this is the part of the corn where much of the masa's color and structure is derived. It is the hardest, most dense part of the kernel. In fact, it's what we're softening the most during the cooking process.

heirloom: Something of intrinsic value that has been passed down from one generation to another. In the case of corn, heirloom seed is genetic material that has been selected, preserved, and passed down through generations.

hybrid: A cross between two or more inbred plants, producing a narrow set of genetic characteristics for more consistent results and higher yield and/or decreased risk.

hydrocolloid: In cooking, a water-soluble polymer used for the purpose of emulsification.

landrace: A more specific designation than *heirloom*, a landrace is a locally adapted, traditional varietal of domesticated species (in the case of corn, a plant) that has developed over time to reflect the natural environment in which it originates; an open-pollinated cultivar that grows through selective breeding.

lime: Also known as quicklime; a white, caustic alkaline substance made of calcium oxide. Derived from limestone that has been heated in an oven through a process called calcination. Once slaked (that is, with the addition of water), lime becomes calcium hydroxide, or cal (also known as pickling lime).

lye: A caustic alkaline solution; the term can refer to either sodium hydroxide or potassium hydroxide.

maíz criollo: Spanish (Mexican) for "native maize." Its literal translation is "creole maize," where *creole* refers to *native* or *indigenous*.

maize: Another word for corn, derived from the Spanish word *maíz*.

maíz nuevo: Spanish for "new corn," referring to corn that has not fully dried and matured, and bears a slightly sweeter flavor.

masa: The Spanish word for dough. In the context of this book, a dough originating in Mesoamerican cuisine, made from ground corn that has been cooked and steeped in an alkaline solution.

masa harina: Spanish for "masa flour," referring to dehydrated masa.

Maseca: A popular brand of masa harina and subsidiary of parent company Gruma.

Mesoamerica: A historic region extending approximately from modern northwestern Mexico to northern Costa Rica. Among the best-known Mesoamerican cultures are the Maya, Mexica (or Aztec), Mixtec, Olmec, Teotihuacan, and Zapotec.

metate: A slightly concave, manual grinding surface, found throughout Mesoamerica, usually composed of basalt. Metates are accompanied by a mano, or rod, composed of the same stone, and were originally used for grinding nixtamal into masa, among other ingredients and uses.

milpa: Derived from the Nahuatl words *milli* ("cultivated land") and *pan* ("in"), milpa is the Spanish word that refers to both a traditional Mesoamerican corn field as well as the system involving the complementary cultivation of corn, beans, and squash (also known as the "three sisters" of agriculture).

molinerx: Gender-neutral Spanish word for a mill operator/artisan (derived from *molinero* and *molinera*).

molino: Spanish for "mill," often one made of basalt stones.

Nahuatl: A group of languages of the Uto-Aztecan language family. Historically the language of the Mexica (Aztecs) and Toltec civilizations, Nahuatl is spoken today in various dialects primarily by the Nahua people within Mexico.

nejayote: Derived from Nuhuatl *nexayotl* (*nextli*, ash; *ayotl*, broth), nejayote is the leftover liquid resulting from nixtamalization. By the time it is ready to be discarded, it contains the alkali water, dirt, and residual bits of corn, including some pericarp, starch, and leached pigments, which increase the viscosity of the solution.

network structure: In reference to masa, the blend of particles that constitute it, including starch, protein, plant tissue, pericarp, and fat. Gums—derived largely from the pericarp—and starch function as the main binders of the network structure, while the protein and plant tissue provide body.

nixtamal: Derived from the Nahuatl word *nextamalli* ("maize soaked in ash water"), this is corn that has gone through the nixtamalization process (that is, been nixtamalized).

nixtamalization: Derived from the Nahuatl words *nextli* ("ash") and *tamalli* ("unformed corn dough" or tamal), the Mesoamerican process of cooking and steeping corn (though other ingredients may technically also be nixtamalized) in an alkaline solution.

pericarp: A corn kernel's skin or hull. When nixtamalized, the pericarp helps retain moisture and encourage pliability in finished masa. When making masa, the aim is to loosen the pericarp from the kernel, activating the corn's natural hemicellulose within the pericarp, which is a key binding agent.

pH: A scale of measure ranging from 0 to 14, with less than 7 being acidic, 7 being neutral, and above 7 being basic or alkaline. (See chart on page 257.)

pozolero: A type of corn traditionally used for pozole.

puff: The result of trapped steam at the center of a tortilla expanding to create a soufflé or ballooning effect.

recipe tortilla: A hybrid, somewhere between a table tortilla and a frying tortilla, that can be used for both tacos and fried applications.

soft endosperm: This is the bright white, soft, chalky substance that you'll find within each corn kernel. The more of this there is relative to the rest of the kernel, the softer the finished masa will be. That said, if there's too much of it, you'll have a hard time achieving an elastic, pliable masa that binds together.

table tortilla: A soft tortilla with a fine grind and high moisture (around 47 percent), which often puffs.

tequesquite: A natural mineral salt with alkaline properties that can be used for nixtamalization and as a leavening agent in masa, among other culinary functions. It is composed primarily of sodium chloride (table salt), sodium bicarbonate (baking soda), potassium carbonate, sodium sulfate, and clay.

tip cap: The top part of a corn kernel where it connects to the cob.

tortilleria: A tortilla bakery.

tortillero: A basket for holding tortillas, often woven (also referred to as a chiquihuite).

tortillerx: Gender-neutral Spanish word for a person who makes tortillas (derived from *tortillero* and *tortillera*).

traditional method: So called in contrast to masa harina, it is the kernel-to-masa process of nixtamalizing corn and grinding the resulting nixtamal with a basalt grinding surface (versus simply adding water to a masa harina).

washoff percentage: The estimated percentage of the corn's pericarp (skin) that is washed off during the nixtamal rinsing process.

Index

V

vegetable oil, smoke point of, 257

vegetables, as toppings and stuffings, 219

W

Waffle, Masa Harina, 249

Wallace, Henry A., 34

Wal-Mart, 71

water, 39

Wells, Pete, 68

White Chocolate Chip Cookies, 250

wood ash nixtamal, 88–89

Acknowledgments

To each and every teacher who has guided this evolving exploration called MASA, I am forever grateful. I'd most like to acknowledge:

The Masienda team—past, present, and future; full-time, part-time, once upon a time; the countless farmers, collaborators, advisors, mentors, partners, from all sides of the border—for creating a space for meaningful cultural conversations like this one to take place. This book would not have been possible without each of your contributions.

Blair Richardson, for your creative guidance throughout every chapter. Jorge Arango, for my earliest masa memory and proposal proofing. Jill Santopietro, for your friendship, resource sharing, and testing.

Andrianna Yeatts, you are truly an equal-opportunity agent. Thank you for your relentless support in bringing this book to the world.

Cristina Garces, our editor, for getting it from the start. Your vision and cheerleading helped make this book the best possible version of itself. Vanessa Dina, our designer, for patiently bringing it all together. And the rest of the team at Chronicle Books: Tera Killip, Steve Kim, Jessica Ling, Magnolia Molcan, Dena Rayess, Keely Thomas-Menter, and Cynthia Shannon.

Michael Graydon, Nikole Herriott, and Kalen Kaminski, for finding creativity, light, and cute—everywhere and in everything. That camera, though ...

Jess Stephens, for your food styling, recipe contributions, and testing.

Selina Pino, for jumping right in, amiga.

Tomas Dávila Rivas, Carlos, y Pedro Reyes Zuñiga, de Molino de Nixtamal El Alaza, por compartir su espacio y experiencia con nosotros.

Iván Vasquez Cruz, Virgilio Vasquez, Yazmín Ramirez Ramirez, y todo el equipo de Agropecuaria Sustentable Chatina, nuestra familia extendida en Oaxaca.

Doña Hilaria Catalina Benito Galvan, Doña Beti Morales Benito, Don Simplicio Morales, Don Juan Velasco, y familia por recibirnos en su casa y compartir su sabiduría.

Sonia Ramírez, Donalda Chávez Ignacio, Gloria Ramírez Hernández, Margarita Martínez Hernández, Victoria Santiago Pacheco de Tacos del Carmen.

Carlos Salgado, Gerardo Gonzalez, Alex Stupak, Daniela Soto-Innes, Karlo Evaristo, Saw Naing, Juan Hernandez, Sean Brock, and Christine Rivera for your thoughtful recipe contributions and collaboration over the years.

Enrique Olvera for helping set this journey into motion.

The Lopez family, Rogelio Lechuga, Azteca Machine Shop, Fernando Ruiz, Rodrigo Ariciega, Gustavo Arellano, Jose Ralat, Lynn Clarkson, Betty Fussell, Jeffrey Pilcher, Harold McGee, Diana Kennedy, Rick and Deann Bayless, CIMMYT, CONABIO, INIFAP, Helbert Almeida-Dominguez, Daniela Soleri, Martha Willcox, Flavio Aragón, Denise Costich, Amado Leyva, Ricardo Muñoz Zurita, Alicia Gironella, Giorgio De'Angeli, Zarela Martinez, Rafael Mier, Patricia Quintana, Elizabeth Dunn, and the folks running the Oregon Nahuatl dictionary—your collective work made researching a true pleasure.

Jody and Jonathan Weiss, for bagging masa, stamping bags, and storing corn.

Dad, for being the earliest supporter of the high masa arts. Mom, for my fondness of proofreading and carnitas.

Danielle Dahlin, for your friendship, encouragement, and loyalty. In the immortal words of Timothy Treadwell, you are a kind warrior.

Julia, my heart, for your unconditional love, unwavering support, and unmatched kindness; for the extra weekends I needed in order to make deadlines, for making space for my books, and letting me keep my writing couch. Most of all, for Luisa.